CHARLES W. QUANTRELL

LECTOR HOUSE PUBLIC DOMAIN WORKS

This book is a result of an effort made by Lector House towards making a contribution to the preservation and repair of original classic literature. The original text is in the public domain in the United States of America, and possibly other countries depending upon their specific copyright laws.

In an attempt to preserve, improve and recreate the original content, certain conventional norms with regard to typographical mistakes, hyphenations, punctuations and/or other related subject matters, have been corrected upon our consideration. However, few such imperfections might not have been rectified as they were inherited and preserved from the original content to maintain the authenticity and construct, relevant to the work. The work might contain a few prior copyright references as well as page references which have been retained, wherever considered relevant to the part of the construct. We believe that this work holds historical, cultural and/or intellectual importance in the literary works community, therefore despite the oddities, we accounted the work for print as a part of our continuing effort towards preservation of literary work and our contribution towards the development of the society as a whole, driven by our beliefs.

We are grateful to our readers for putting their faith in us and accepting our imperfections with regard to preservation of the historical content. We shall strive hard to meet up to the expectations to improve further to provide an enriching reading experience.

Though, we conduct extensive research in ascertaining the status of copyright before redeveloping a version of the content, in rare cases, a classic work might be incorrectly marked as not-in-copyright. In such cases, if you are the copyright holder, then kindly contact us or write to us, and we shall get back to you with an immediate course of action.

HAPPY READING!

CHARLES W. QUANTRELL

JOHN P. BURCH,
HARRISON TROW

ISBN: 978-93-5614-695-2

Published: 1923

LECTOR HOUSE LLP
E-MAIL: info@lectorhouse.com

CHARLES W. QUANTRELL

A TRUE HISTORY OF HIS GUERRILLA WARFARE ON THE MISSOURI AND KANSAS BORDER DURING THE CIVIL WAR OF 1861 TO 1865

BY

JOHN P. BURCH

ILLUSTRATED

AS TOLD BY
CAPTAIN HARRISON TROW

ONE WHO FOLLOWED QUANTRELL THROUGH HIS WHOLE COURSE

1923

CHARLES W. QUANTRELL

CAPTAIN HARRISON TROW

CONTENTS

INTRODUCTION

CAPTAIN HARRISON TROW, who will be eighty years old this coming October, was with Quantrell during the whole of the conflict from 1861 to 1865, and for the past twenty years I have been at him to give his consent for me to write a true history of the Quantrell Band, until at last he has given it.

This narrative was written just as he told it to me, giving accounts of fights that he participated in, narrow escapes experienced, dilemmas it seemed almost impossible to get out of, and also other battles; the life of the James boys and Youngers as they were with Quantrell during the war, and after the war, when they became outlaws by publicity of the daily newspapers, being accused of things which they never did and which were laid at their feet.

Captain Trow identified Jesse James when the latter was killed at St. Joseph. He also was the last man to surrender in the State of Missouri.

JOHN P. BURCH.

THE AUTHOR

CAPTAIN HARRISON TROW was born in Pittsburgh, Pennsylvania, October 16, 1843, moved to Illinois in 1848, and thence to Missouri in 1850, and went to Hereford, Texas, in 1901, where he now resides. At the age of nine years, he, having one of the nicest, neatest and sweetest stepmothers (as they all are), and things not being as pleasant at home as they should be (which is often the case where there is a stepmother), and getting all the peach tree sprouts for the whole family used on him, he decided the world was too large for him to take such treatment, and one day he proceeded to give the stepmother a good flogging, such as he had been getting, and left for brighter fields.

In a few days he made his way to Independence, Missouri, got into a game of marbles, playing keeps, in front of a blacksmith shop, and won seventy-five cents. Then and there Uncle George Hudsbath rode up and wanted to hire a hand. Young Trow jumped at the job and talked to Mr. Hudsbath a few minutes and soon was up behind him and riding away to his new home. Young Trow proved to be the lad Uncle George was looking for and stayed with him until the war broke out.

THE FALSE JONAH

EARLY in the year of 1861, about in January, Jim Lane sent a false Jonah down to Missouri to investigate the location of the negroes and stock, preparing to make a raid within a short time. This Jonah located first at Judge Gray's house at Bone Hill, was fed by Judge Gray's "niggers" and was secreted in an empty ice house where they kept ice in the summer time. He would come out in the night time and plan with the "niggers" for their escape into Kansas with the horses, buggies and carriages and other valuables belonging to their master that they could get possession of. But an old negro woman, old Maria by name, gave the Jonah away.

Chat Rennick, one of the neighbors, and two other men secreted themselves in the negroes' cabin so as to hear what he was telling the negroes. After he had made all his plans for their escape Chat Rennick came out on him with the other two men and took him prisoner and started north to the Missouri River. Securing a skiff, they floated out into the river and when in about the center there came up a heavy gale, and one of these gentlemen thought it best to unload part of the cargo, so he was thrown overboard. As for the negroes, they repented in sack cloth and ashes and all stayed at home and took care of their master and mistress, as Jonah did in the olden times. As for the Jonah, I do not know whether the fish swallowed him or not, but if one did he did not get sick and throw him up. This took place at my wife's uncle's home, Judge James Gray.

EARLY LIFE OF QUANTRELL

THE early life of Quantrell was obscure and uneventful. He was born near Hagerstown, Maryland, July 20, 1836, and was reared there until he was sixteen years of age. He remained always an obedient and affectionate son. His mother had been left a widow when he was only a few years old.

For some time preceding 1857, Quantrell's only brother lived in Kansas. He wrote to his younger brother, Charles, to come there, and after his arrival they decided on a trip to California. About the middle of the summer of 1857 the two started for California with a freight outfit. Upon reaching Little Cottonwood River, Kansas, they decided to camp for the night. This they did. All was going well. After supper twenty-one outlaws, or Redlegs, belonging to Jim Lane at Lawrence, Kansas, rode up and killed the elder brother, wounded Charles, and took everything in sight, money, and even the "nigger" who went with them to do the cooking. They thought more of the d— —d "nigger" than they did of all the rest of the loot. They left poor Charles there to die and be eaten later by wolves or some other wild animal that might come that way. Poor Charles lay there for three days before anyone happened by, guarding his dead brother, suffering near death from his wounds. After three days an old Shawnee Indian named Spye Buck came along, buried the elder brother and took Charles to his home and nursed him back to life and strength. After six months to a year Charles Quantrell was able to go at ease, and having a good education for those days, got a school and taught until he had earned enough money to pay the old Indian for keeping him while he was sick and to get him to Lawrence. He reached Lawrence and went to where Jim Lane was stationed with his company. He wanted to get into the company that murdered his brother and wounded himself. After a few days he was taken in and, from outward appearance, he became a full-fledged Redleg, but in his heart he was doing this only to seek revenge on those who had killed his brother and wounded him at Cottonwood, Kansas.

Quantrell, now known as Charles Hart, became intimate with Lane and ostensibly attached himself to the fortunes of the anti-slavery party. In order to attain his object and get a step nearer his goal, it became necessary for him to speak of John Brown. He always spoke of him to General Lane, who was at that time Colonel Lane, in command of a regiment at Lawrence, as one for whom he had great admiration. Quantrell became enrolled in a company that held all but two of the men who had done the deadly work at Cottonwood, Kansas. First as a private, then as an orderly and sergeant, Quantrell soon gained the esteem of his officers and the confidence of his men.

One day Quantrell and three men were sent down in the neighborhood of Wyandotte to meet a wagon load of "niggers" coming up to Missouri under the pilotage of Jack Winn, a somewhat noted horse thief and abolutionist. One of the three men failed to return with Quantrell, nor could any account be given of his absence until his body was found near a creek several days afterwards. In the center of his forehead was the round, smooth hole of a navy revolver bullet. Those who looked for Jack Winn's safe arrival were also disappointed. People traveling the road passed the corpse almost daily and the buzzards found it first, and afterwards the curious. There was the same round hole in the forehead and the same sure mark of the navy revolver bullet. This thing went on for several months, scarcely a week passing but that some sentinel was found dead at his post, some advance picket surprised and shot at his outpost watch station.

The men began to whisper, one to another, and to cast about for the cavalry Jonah who was in their midst. One company alone, that of Captain Pickins, the company to which Quantrell belonged, had lost thirteen men between October, 1859 and 1860. Other companies had lost two to three each. A railroad conductor named Rogers had been shot through the forehead. Quantrell and Pickens became intimate, as a captain and lieutenant of the same company should, and confided many things to each other. One night the story of the Cottonwood River was told and Pickens dwelt with just a little relish upon it. Three days later Pickens and two of his most reliable men were found dead on Bull Creek, shot like the balance, in the middle of the forehead. For a time after Pickens' death there was a lull in the constant conscription demanded by the Nemesis. The new lieutenant bought himself a splendid uniform, owned the best horse in the territory and instead of one navy revolver, now had two. Organizations of all sorts now sprang up, Free Soil clubs, Men of Equal Rights, Sons of Liberty, Destroying Angels, Lane's Loyal Leaguers, and everyone made haste to get his name signed to both constitution and by-laws.

Lawrence especially effected the Liberator Club, whose undivided mission was to found freedom for all the slaves now in Missouri.

Quantrell persevered in his efforts to kill all of the men who had had a hand in the killing of his brother and the wounding of himself. With this in view, he induced seven Liberators to co-operate with him in an attack on Morgan Walker. These seven men whom Quantrell picked were the last except two of the men he had sworn vengeance upon when left to die at Cottonwood River, Kansas. He told them that Morgan Walker had a lot of "niggers," horses and cattle and money and that the sole purpose was to rob and kill him. Quantrell's only aim was to get these seven men. Morgan Walker was an old citizen of Jackson County, a venerable pioneer who had settled there when buffalo grazed on the prairie beyond Westport and where, in the soft sands beyond the inland streams, there were wolf and moccasin tracks. This man, Morgan Walker, was the man Quantrell had proposed to rob. He lived some five or six miles from Independence and owned about twenty negroes of various ages and sizes. The probabilities were that a skillfully conducted raid might leave him without a "nigger."

Well mounted and armed, the little detachment left Lawrence quietly, rode two by two, far apart, until the first rendezvous was reached, a clump of timber at a ford on Indian Creek. It was the evening of the second day, and they tarried long enough to rest their horses and eat a hearty supper.

Before daylight the next morning the entire party were hidden in some heavy timber about two miles west of Walker's house. There these seven men stayed, none of them stirring, except Quantrell. Several times during the day, however, he went backwards and forwards, apparently to the fields where the negroes were at work, and whenever he returned he brought something either for the horses or the men to eat.

Mr. Walker had two sons, and before it was yet night, these boys and their father were seen putting into excellent order their double-barrel shotguns, and a little later three neighbors who likewise carried double-barrel shotguns rode up to the house. Quantrell, who brought news of many other things to his comrades, brought no note of this. If he saw it he made no sign. When Quantrell arranged his men for the dangerous venture they were to proceed, first to the house, gain access to it, capture all the male members of the family and put them under guard, assemble all the negroes and make them hitch up the horses to the wagons and then gallop them for Kansas. Fifty yards from the gate the eight men dismounted and fastened their horses, and the march to the house began. Quantrell led. He was very cool and seemed to see everything. The balance of his men had their revolvers in their hands while he had his in his belt. Quantrell knocked loudly at the oaken panel of the door. No answer. He knocked again and stood perceptibly at one side. Suddenly the door flared open and Quantrell leaped into the hall with a bound like a red deer. A livid sheet of flame burst out through the darkness where he had disappeared, followed by another as the second barrels of the guns were discharged and the tragedy was over. Six fell where they stood, riddled with buckshot. One staggered to the garden and died there. The seventh, hard hit and unable to mount his horse, dragged himself to a patch of timber and waited for the dawn. They tracked him by the blood upon the leaves and found him early in the morning. Another volley, and the last Liberator was liberated.

Walker and his two sons, assisted by three of the stalwart and obliging neighbors, had done a clean night's work, and a righteous one. This being the last of the Redlegs, except two, who murdered Quantrell's brother and wounded him in Cottonwood, Kansas, in 1857, he closed his eyes and ears from ever being a scout for old Jim Lane any more.

In a few days after the ambuscade at Walker's, Charles W. Quantrell, instead of Charles Hart, as he was known, then was not afraid to tell his name on Missouri soil. He wrote to Jim Lane, telling him what had happened to the scouts sent out by him, and as the war was on then, Quantrell told Lane in his letter that he was going to Richmond, Virginia, to get a commission from under Jeff Davis' own hand, which he did (as you will read further on in this narrative), to operate on the border at will. So Quantrell, being fully equipped with all credentials, notified Jim Lane of Missouri, telling him he would treat him with the same or better courtesy than he (Lane) had treated him and his brother at Cottonwood River, Kansas, in 1857. This made Jim Lane mad, and he began to send his roving, robbing, and thieving bands into Missouri, and Charles W. Quantrell, having a band of well organized guerrillas of about fifty men, began to play on their golden harps. Every time they came in sight, which was almost every day, they would have a fight to the finish.

WHY THE QUANTRELL GUERRILLAS WERE ORGANIZED

IT all came about from the Redlegs or Kansas Jayhawkers. For two years Kansas hated Missouri and at all times during these two years there were Redlegs from old Jim Lane's army crossing to Missouri, stealing everything they could get their hands on, driving stock, insulting innocent women and children, and hanging and killing old men; so it is the province of history to deal with results, not to condemn the phenomena which produce them. Nor has it the right to decry the instruments Providence always raises up in the midst of great catastrophes to restore the equilibrium of eternal justice. Civil War might well have made the Guerrilla, but only the excesses of civil war could have made him the untamable and unmerciful creature that history finds him. When he first went into the war he was somewhat imbued with the old-fashioned belief that soldiering meant fighting and that fighting meant killing. He had his own ideas of soldiering, however, and desired nothing so much as to remain at home and meet its despoilers upon his own premises. Not naturally cruel, and averse to invading the territory of any other people, he could not understand the patriotism of those who invaded his own territory. Patriotism, such as he was required to profess, could not spring up in the market place at the bidding of Redleg or Jayhawker. He believed, indeed, that the patriotism of Jim Lane and Jennison was merely a highway robbery transferred from the darkness to the dawn, and he believed the truth. Neither did the Guerrilla become merciless all of a sudden. Pastoral in many cases by profession, and reared among the bashful and timid surroundings of agricultural life, he knew nothing of the tiger that was in him until death had been dashed against his eyes in numberless and brutal ways, and until the blood of his own kith and kin had been sprinkled plentifully upon things that his hands touched, and things that entered into his daily existence. And that fury of ideas also came to him slowly, which is more implacable than the fury of men, for men have heart, and opinion has none. It took him likewise some time to learn that the Jayhawkers' system of saving the Union was a system of brutal force, which bewailed not even that which it crushed; and it belied its doctrine by its tyranny, stained its arrogated right by its violence, and dishonored its vaunted struggles by its executions. But blood is as contagious as air. The fever of civil war has its delirium.

When the Guerrilla awoke he was a giant! He took in, as it were, and at a single glance, all the immensity of the struggle. He saw that he was hunted and proscribed; that he had neither a flag nor a government; that the rights and the amenities of civilized warfare were not to be his; that a dog's death was certain to be his if he surrendered even in the extremest agony of battle; that the house which sheltered him had to be burned; the father who succored him had to be butchered; the mother who prayed for him had to be insulted; the sister who carried him food had to be imprisoned; the neighborhood which witnessed his combats had to be laid waste; the comrade shot down by his side had to be put to death as a wild beast—and he lifted up the black flag in self-defense and fought as became a free man and a hero.

Much obloquy has been cast upon the Guerrilla organization because in its name bad men plundered the helpless, pillaged the friend and foe alike, assaulted non-combatants and murdered the unresisting and the innocent. Such devils' work was not Guerrilla work. It fitted all too well the hands of those cowards crouching in the rear of either army and courageous only where women defended what remained to themselves and their children. Desperate and remorseless as he undoubtedly was, the Guerrilla saw shining upon his pathway a luminous patriotism, and he followed it eagerly that he might kill in the name of God and his country. The nature of his warfare made him responsible, of course, for many monstrous things he had no personal share in bringing about. Denied a hearing at the bar of public opinion, of all the loyal journalists, painted blacker than ten devils, and given a countenance that was made to retain some shadow of all the death agonies he had seen, is it strange in the least that his fiendishness became omnipresent as well as omnipotent? To justify one crime on the part of a Federal soldier, five crimes more cruel were laid at the door of the Guerrilla. His long gallop not only tired, but infuriated his hunters. That savage standing at bay and dying always as a wolf dies when barked at by hounds and dudgeoned by countrymen, made his enemies fear and hate him. Hence, from all their bomb-proofs his slanderers fired silly lies at long range, and put afloat unnatural stories that hurt him only as it deepened the savage intensity of an already savage strife. Save in rare and memorable instances, the Guerrilla murdered only when fortune in open and honorable battle gave into his hands some victims who were denied that death in combat which they afterward found by ditch or lonesome roadside. Man for man, he put his life fairly on the cast of the war dice, and died when the need came as the red Indian dies, stoical and grim as a stone.

As strange as it may seem, the perilous fascination of fighting under a black flag—where the wounded could have neither surgeon nor hospital, and where all that remained to the prisoners was the absolute certainty of speedy death—attracted a number of young men to the various Guerrilla bands, gently nurtured, born to higher destinies, capable of sustaining exertion in any scheme or enterprise, and fit for callings high up in the scale of science or philosophy. Others came who had deadly wrongs to avenge, and these gave to all their combats that sanguinary hue which still remains a part of the Guerrilla's legacy. Almost from the first a large majority of Quantrell's original command had over them the shadow of some terrible crime. This one recalled a father murdered, this one a brother waylaid and shot, this one a house pillaged and burned, this one a relative assassinated, this one a grievous insult while at peace at home, this one a robbery of all his earthly possessions, this one the force that compelled him to witness the brutal treatment of a mother or sister, this one was driven away from his own like a thief in the night, this one was threatened with death for opinion's sake, this one was proscribed at the instance of some designing neighbor, this one was arrested wantonly and forced to do the degrading work of a menial; while all had more or less of wrath laid up against the day when they were to meet, face to face and hand to hand, those whom they had good cause to regard as the living embodiment of unnumbered wrongs. Honorable soldiers in the Confederate army—amenable to every generous impulse and exact in the performance of every manly duty—deserted even the ranks which they had adorned and became desperate Guerillas because the home they had left had been given to the flames, or a gray-haired father shot upon his own hearthstone. They wanted to avoid the uncertainty of regular battle and know by actual results how many died as a propitation or a sacrifice. Every other passion became subsidiary to that of revenge. They sought personal encounters that their own handiwork might become unmistakably manifest. Those who died by other agencies than their own were not counted in the general summing up of the fight, nor were the solacements of any victory sweet to them unless they had the knowledge of being important factors in its achievement.

As this class of Guerrilla increased, the warfare of the border became necessarily more cruel and unsparing. Where at first there was only killing in ordinary battle, there came to be no quarter shown. The wounded of the enemy next felt the might of this individual vengeance—acting through a community of bitter memories—and from every stricken field there began, by and by, to come up the substance of this awful bulletin: Dead, such and such a number; *wounded, none*. The war had then passed into its fever heat, and thereafter the gentle and the merciful, equally with the harsh and the revengeful, spared nothing clad in blue that could be captured.

QUANTRELL'S FIRST BATTLE IN THE CIVIL WAR

QUANTRELL, together with Captain Blunt, returned from Richmond, Virginia, in the fall of 1861, with his commission from under the hand of Jeff Davis, to operate at will along the Kansas border. He began to organize his band of Guerrillas. His first exploits were confined to but eight men. These eight men were William Haller, James and John Little, Edward Koger, Andrew Walker, son of Morgan Walker, at whose farm Quantrell got rid of the last but two of the band that murdered his brother at Cottonwood River, Kansas, and left himself to die; John Hampton James Kelley and Solomon Bashman.

This little band knew nothing whatever of war, and knew only how to fight and shoot. They lived on the border and had some old scores to settle with the Jayhawkers.

These eight men, or rather nine—for Quantrell commanded—encountered their first hereditary enemies, the Jayhawkers. Lane entered Missouri only on grand occasions; Jennison only once in a while as on a frolic. One was a collossal thief; the other a picayune one. Lane dealt in mules by herds, horses by droves, wagons by parks, negroes by neighborhoods, household effects by the ton, and miscellaneous plunder by the cityful; Jennison contented himself with the pocket-books of his prisoners, the pin money of the women, and the wearing apparel of the children. Lane was a real prophet of demagogism, with insanity latent in his blood; Jennison a *sans coulotte,* who, looking upon himself as a bastard, sought to become legitimate by becoming brutal.

It was in the vicinity of Morgan Walker's that Quantrell, with his little command, ambushed a portion of Jennison's regiment and killed five of his thieves, getting some good horses, saddles and bridles and revolvers. The next fight occurred upon the premises of Volney Ryan, a citizen of Jackson County, with a company of Missouri militia, a company of militia notorious for three things—robbing hen roosts, stealing horses, and running away from the enemy. The eight Guerrillas struck them just at daylight, charged through it, charged back again, and when they returned from the pursuit they counted fifteen dead, the fruits of a running battle.

An old man by the name of Searcy, claiming to be a Southern man, was stealing all over Jackson County and using violence here and there when he could not succeed through persuasion. Quantrell swooped down upon him one afternoon, tried him that night and hanged him the next morning, four Guerrillas dragging on the rope. Seventy-five head of horses were found in the dead man's possession, all belonging to the citizens of the county, and any number of deeds to small tracts of land, notes and mortgages, and private accounts. All were returned. The execution acted as a thunder-storm. It restored the equilibrium of the moral atmosphere. The border warfare had found a chief.

The eight Guerrillas had now grown to fifty. Among the new recruits were David Poole, John Jarrette, William Coger, Richard Burns, George Todd, George Shephers, Coleman Younger, myself and several others of like enterprise and daring. An organization was at once effected, and Quantrell was made captain; William Haller, first lieutenant; William Gregg, second; George Todd, third, and John Jarrette, orderly sergeant. The eagles were beginning to congregate.

Poole, an unschooled Aristophanes of the Civil War, laughed at calamity, and mocked when any man's fear came. But for its picturesqueness, his speech would have been comedy personified. He laughed loudest when he was deadliest, and treated fortune with no more dignity in one extreme than in another. Gregg, a grim Saul among the Guerrillas, made of the Confederacy a mistress, and like the Douglass of old, was ever tender and true to her. Jarrette, the man who never knew fear, added to fearlessness and immense activity an indomitable will. He was a soldier in the saddle *par excellence*. John Coger never missed a battle nor a bullet. Wounded thirteen times, he lived as an exemplification of what a Guerrilla could endure—the amount of lead he could comfortably get along with and keep fat. Steadfastness was his test of merit—comradeship his point of honor. He who had John Coger at his back had a mountain. Todd was the incarnate devil of battle. He thought of fighting when awake, dreamed of it at night, mingled talk of it in laxation, and went hungry many a day and shelterless many a night that he might find his enemy and have his fill of fight. Quantrell always had to hold him back, and yet he was his thunderbolt. He discussed nothing in the shape of orders. A soldier who discusses is like a hand which would think. He only charged. Were he attacked in front—a charge; were he attacked in the rear—a charge; on either flank—a charge. Finally, in a desperate charge, and doing a hero's work upon the stricken rear of the Second Colorado, he was killed. This was George Todd. Shepherd, a patient, cool, vigilant leader, knew all the roads and streams, all the fords and passes, all modes of egress and ingress, all safe and dangerous places, all the treacherous non-combatants, and all the trustworthy ones—everything indeed that the few needed to know who were fighting the many. In addition, there were few among the Guerrillas who were better pistol shots. It used to do Quantrell good to see him in the skirmish line. Coleman Younger, a boy having still about his neck the purple marks of a rope made the night when the Jayhawkers shot down his old father and strung him up to a blackjack, spoke rarely, and was away a great deal in the woods. "What was he doing?" his companions began to ask one of another. He had a mission to perform—he was pistol practicing. Soon he was perfect, and then he laughed often and talked a good deal. There had come to him now that intrepid gaiety that plays with death. He changed devotion to his family into devotion to his country, and he fought and killed with the conscience of a hero.

FIGHT AT CHARLES YOUNGER'S FARM

THE new organization was about to be baptized. Burris, raiding generally along the Missouri border, had a detachment foraging in the neighborhood of Charles Younger's farm. This Charles Younger was an uncle of Coleman, and he lived within three miles of Independence, Missouri, the county seat of Jackson County. The militia detachment numbered eighty-four and the Guerrillas thirty-two. At sunset Quantrell struck their camp. Forewarned of his coming, they were already in line. One volley settled them. Five fell at the first fire and seven more were killed in the chase. The shelter of Independence alone, where the balance of the regiment was as a breakwater saved the detachment from utter extinction. On this day—the 10th of November, 1861—Cole Younger killed a militiaman seventy-one measured yards. The pistol practice was bearing fruit.

Independence was essentially a city of fruits and flowers. About every house there was a *parterre* and contiguous to every *parterre* there was an orchard. Built where the woods and the prairies met, when it was most desirable there was sunlight, and when it was most needed there was shade. The war found it rich, prosperous and contented, and it left it as an orange that had been devoured. Lane hated it because it was a hive of secession, and Jennison preyed upon it because Guerrilla bees flew in and out. On one side the devil, on the other the deep sea. Patriotism, that it might not be tempted, ran the risk very often of being drowned. Something also of Spanish intercourse and connection belonged to it. Its square was a plaza; its streets centered there; its courthouse was a citadel. Truer people never occupied a town; braver fathers never sent their sons to war; grander matrons never prayed to God for right, and purer women never waited through it all—the siege, the sack, the pillage and the battle—for the light to break in the East at last, the end to come in fate's own good and appointed time.

FIGHT AT INDEPENDENCE

QUANTRELL had great admiration for Independence; his men adored it. Burris' regiment was still there—fortified in the courthouse—and one day in February, 1862, the Guerrillas charged the town. It was a desperate assault. Quantrell and Poole dashed down one street. Cole Younger and Todd down another, Gregg and Shepherd down a third, Haller, Coger, Burns, Walker and others down the balance of the approaches to the square. Behind heavy brick walls the militia, of course, fought and fought, besides, at a great advantage. Save seven surprised in the first moments of the rapid onset and shot down, none others were killed, and Quantrell was forced to retire from the town, taking some necessary ordnance, quartermaster and commissary supplies from the stores under the very guns of the courthouse. None of his men were killed, though as many as eleven were wounded. This was the initiation of Independence into the mysteries as well as the miseries of border warfare, and thereafter and without a month of cessation, it was to get darker and darker for the beautiful town.

Swinging back past Independence from the east the day after it had been charged, Quantrell moved up in the neighborhood of Westport and put scouts upon the roads leading to Kansas City. Two officers belonging to Jennison's regiment were picked up—a lieutenant, who was young, and a captain, who was of middle age. They had only time to pray. Quantrell always gave time for this, and had always performed to the letter the last commissions left by those who were doomed. The lieutenant did not want to pray. "It could do no good," he said. "God knew about as much concerning the disposition it was intended to be made of his soul as he could suggest to him." The captain took a quarter of an hour to make his peace. Both were shot. Men commonly die at God's appointed time, beset by Guerrillas, suddenly and unawares. Another of the horrible surprises of Civil War.

At first, and because of Quantrell's presence, Kansas City swarmed like an ant hill during a rainstorm; afterwards, and when the dead officers were carried in, like a firebrand had been cast thereon.

SECOND FIGHT AT INDEPENDENCE

WHILE at the house of Charles Cowherd, a courier came up with the information that Independence, which had not been garrisoned for some little time, was again in possession of a company of militia. Another attack was resolved upon. On the night of February 20, 1862, Quantrell marched to the vicinity of the town and waited there for daylight. The first few faint streaks in the East constituted the signal. There was a dash altogether down South Main Street, a storm of cheers and bullets, a roar of iron feet on the rocks of the roadway, and the surprise was left to work itself out. It did, and reversely. Instead of the one company reported in possession of the town, four were found, numbering three hundred men. They manned the courthouse in a moment, made of its doors an eruption and of its windows a tempest, killed a noble Guerrilla, young George, shot Quantrell's horse from under him, held their own everywhere and held the fort. As before, all who were killed among the Federals, and they lost seventeen, were those killed in the first few moments of the charge. Those who hurried alive into the courthouse were safe. Young George, dead in his first battle, had all the promise of a bright career. None rode further nor faster in the charge, and when he fell he fell so close to the fence about the fortified building that it was with difficulty his comrades took his body out from under a point blank fire and bore it off in safety.

It was a part of Quantrell's tactics to disband every now and then. "Scattered soldiers," he argued, "make a scattered trail. The regiment that has but one man to hunt can never find him." The men needed heavier clothing and better horses, and the winter, more than ordinarily severe, was beginning to tell. A heavy Federal force was also concentrating in Kansas City, ostensibly to do service along the Missouri River, but really to drive out of Jackson County a Guerrilla band that under no circumstances at that time could possibly have numbered over fifty. Quantrell, therefore, for an accumulation of reasons, ordered a brief disbandment. It had hardly been accomplished before Independence swapped a witch for a devil. Burris evacuated the town; Jennison occupied it. In his regiment were trappers who trapped for dry goods; fishermen who fished for groceries. At night passers-by were robbed of their pocketbooks; in the morning, market women of their meat baskets. Neither wiser, perhaps, nor better than the Egyptians, the patient and all-suffering citizens had got rid of the lean kine in order to make room for the lice.

FLANKED INDEPENDENCE

AT the appointed time, and at the place of David George, the assembling was as it should be. Quantrell meant to attack Jennison in Independence and destroy him if possible, and so moved in that direction as far as Little Blue Church. Here he met Allen Parmer, a regular red Indian of a scout, who never forgot to count a column or know the line of march of an enemy, and Parmer reported that instead of three hundred Jayhawkers being in Independence there were six hundred. Too many for thirty-two men to grapple, and fortified at that, they all said. It would be murder in the first degree and unnecessary murder in addition. Quantrell, forego-ing with a struggle the chance to get at his old acquaintance of Kansas, flanked Independence and stopped for a night at the residence of Zan Harris, a true Southern man and a keen observer of passing events. Early the next morning he crossed the Big Blue at the bridge on the main road to Kansas City, surprised and shot down a detachment of thirteen Federals watching it, burned the structure to the water, and marched rapidly on in a southwest direction, leaving Westport to the right. At noon the command was at the residence of Alexander Majors.

FIGHT AT TATE HOUSE

AFTER the meal at Major's Quantrell resumed his march, sending Haller and Todd ahead with an advance guard and bringing up the rear himself with the main body of twenty-two men. Night overtook him at the Tate House, three miles east of Little Santa Fe, a small town in Jackson County, close to the Kansas line, and he camped there. Haller and Todd were still further along, no communication being established between these two parts of a common whole. The day had been cold and the darkness bitter. That weariness that comes with a hard ride, a rousing fire, and a hearty supper, fell early upon the Guerrillas. One sentinel at the gate kept drowsy watch, and the night began to deepen. In various attitudes and in various places, twenty-one of the twenty-two men were sound asleep, the twenty-second keeping watch and ward at the gate in freezing weather.

It was just twelve o'clock and the fire in the capacious fireplace was burning low. Suddenly a shout was heard. The well known challenge of "Who are you?" arose on the night air, followed by a pistol shot, and then a volley. Quantrell, sleeping always like a cat, shook himself loose from his blankets and stood erect in the glare of the firelight. Three hundred Federals, following all day on his trail, had marked him take cover at night and went to bag him, boots and breeches. They had hitched their horses back in the brush and stole upon the dwelling afoot. So noiseless had been their advance, and so close were they upon the sentinel before they were discovered, that he had only time to cry out, fire, and rush for the timber. He could not get back to his comrades, for some Federals were between him and the door. As he ran he received a volley, but in the darkness he escaped.

The house was surrounded. To the men withinside this meant, unless they could get out, death by fire and sword. Quantrell was trapped, he who had been accorded the fox's cunning and the panther's activity. He glided to the window and looked out cautiously. The cold stars above shone, and the blue figures under them and on every hand seemed colossal. The fist of a heavy man struck the door hard, and a deep voice commanded, "Make a light." There had been no firing as yet, save the shot of the sentinel and its answering volley. Quantrell went quietly to all who were still asleep and bade them get up and get ready. It was the moment when death had to be looked in the face. Not a word was spoken. The heavy fist was still hammering at the door. Quantrell crept to it on tip-toe, listened a second at the sounds outside and fired. "Oh," and a stalwart Federal fell prone across the porch, dying. "You asked for a light and you got it, d— —n you," Quantrell ejaculated, cooler than his pistol barrel. Afterwards there was no more bravado. "Bar the doors and barricade the windows," he shouted; "quick, men!" Beds were freely used and applicable furniture. Little and Shepherd stood by one door; Jarrette, Younger, Toler and Hoy barricaded the other and made the windows bullet-proof. Outside the Federal fusilade was incessant. Mistaking Tate's house for a frame house, when it was built of brick, the commander of the enemy could be heard encouraging his men to shoot low and riddle the building. Presently there was a lull, neither party firing for the space of several minutes, and Quantrell spoke to his people: "Boys, we are in a tight place. We can't stay here, and I do not mean to surrender. All who want to follow me out can say so. I will do the best I can for them." Four concluded to appeal to the Federals for protection; seventeen to follow Quantrell to the death. He called a parley, and informed the Federal commander that four of his followers wanted to surrender. "Let them come out," was the order. Out they went, and the fight began again. Too eager to see what manner of men their prisoners were, the Federals holding the west side of the house huddled about them eagerly. Ten Guerrillas from the upper story fired at the crowd and brought down six. A roar followed this, and a rush back again to cover at the double quick. It was hot work now. Quantrell, supported by James Little, Cole Younger, Hoy and Stephen Shores held the upper story, while Jarrette, Toler, George Shepherd and others held the lower. Every shot told. The proprietor of the house, Major Tate, was a Southern hero, gray-headed, but Roman. He went about laughing. "Help me get my family out, boys," he said, "and I will help you hold the house. It's about as good a time for me to die, I reckon, as any other, if so be that God wills it. But the old woman is only a woman." Another parley. Would the Federal officer let the women and children out? Yes, gladly, and the old man, too. There was eagerness for this, and much of veritable cunning. The family occupied an ell of the mansion with which there was no communication from the main building where Quantrell and his men were, save by way of a door which opened upon a porch, and this porch was under the concentrating fire of the assailants. After the family moved out the attacking party would throw skirmishers in and then—the torch. Quantrell understood it in a moment and spoke up to the father of the family: "Go out, Major. It is your duty to be with your wife and children." The old man went, protesting. Perhaps for forty years the blood had not coursed so rapidly and so pleasantly through his veins. Giving ample time for the family to get safely beyond the range of the fire of the besieged, Quantrell went back to his post and looked out. He saw two Federals standing together beyond revolver range. "Is there a shotgun here?" he asked. Cole Younger brought him one loaded with buckshot. Thrusting half his body out the nearest window, and receiving as many volleys as there were sentinels, he fired the two barrels of his gun so near together that they sounded as one barrel. Both Federals fell, one dead, the other mortally wounded. Following this daring and conspicuous feat there went up a yell so piercing and exultant that even the horses, hitched in the timber fifty yards away, reared in their fright and snorted in terror. Black columns of smoke blew past the windows where the Guerrillas were, and a bright red flame leaped up towards the sky on the wings of the wind. The ell of the house had been fired and was burning fiercely. Quantrell's face—just a little paler than usual—had a set look that was not good to see. The tiger was at bay. Many of the men's revolvers were empty, and in order to gain time to reload them, another parley was held. The talk was of surrender. The Federal commander demanded immediate submission, and Shepherd, with a voice heard above the rage and the roar of the flames, pleaded for twenty minutes. No. Ten? No. Five? No. Then the commander cried out in a voice not a whit inferior to Shepherd's in compass: "You have one minute. If, at its expiration, you have not surrendered, not a single man among you shall escape alive." "Thank you," said Cole Younger, *soto voce*, "catching comes before hanging." "Count sixty, then, and be d— —d to you"! Shepherd shouted as a parting volley, and then a strange silence fell upon all these desperate men face to face with imminent death. When every man was ready, Quantrell said briefly, "Shot guns to the front." Six loaded heavily with buck shot, were borne there, and he put himself at the head of the six men who carried them. Behind these those having only revolvers. In single file, the charging column was formed in the main room of the building. The glare of the burning ell lit it up as though the sun was shining there. Some tightened their pistol belts. One fell upon his knees and prayed. Nobody scoffed at him, for God was in that room. He is everywhere when heroes confess. There were seventeen about to receive the fire of three hundred.

Ready! Quantrell flung the door wide open and leaped out. The shotgun men—Jarrette, Younger, Shepherd, Toler, Little and Hoy, were hard behind him. Right and left from the thin short column a fierce fire beat into the very faces of the Federals, who recoiled in some confusion, shooting, however, from every side. There was a yell and a grand rush, and when the end had come and all the fixed realities figured up, the enemy had eighteen killed, twenty-nine badly wounded; and five prisoners, and the captured horses of the Guerrillas. Not a man of Quantrell's band was touched, as it broke through the cordon on the south of the house and gained the sheltering timber beyond. Hoy, as he rushed out the third from Quantrell and fired both barrels of his gun, was so near to a stalwart Federal that he knocked him over the head with a musket and rendered him senseless. To capture him afterwards was like capturing a dead man. But little pursuit was attempted. Quantrell halted at the timber, built a fire, reloaded every gun and pistol, and took a philosophical view of the situation. Enemies were all about him. He had lost five men—four of whom, however, he was glad to get rid of—and the balance were afoot. Patience! He had just escaped from an environment sterner than any yet spread for him, and fortune was not apt to offset one splendid action by another exactly opposite. Choosing, therefore, a rendezvous upon the head waters of the Little Blue, another historic stream of Jackson County, he reached the residence of David Wilson late the next morning, after a forced march of great exhaustion. The balance of the night, however, had still to be one of surprises and counter-surprises, not alone to the Federals, but to the other portion of Quantrell's command under Haller and Todd.

Encamped four miles south of Tate House, the battle there had roused them instantly. Getting to saddle quickly, they were galloping back to the help of their comrades when a Federal force, one hundred strong, met them full in the road. Some minutes of savage fighting ensued, but Haller could not hold his own with thirteen men, and he retreated, firing, to the brush.

Afterwards everything was made plain. The four men who surrendered so abjectly at the Tate house imagined that it would bring help to their condition if they told all they knew, and they told without solicitation the story of Haller's advance and the whereabouts of his camp. A hundred men were instantly dispatched to surprise it or storm it, but the firing had roused the isolated Guerrillas, and they got out in safety after a rattling fight of some twenty minutes.

FIGHT AT CLARK'S HOME

IN April, 1862, Quantrell, with seventeen men, was camped at the residence of Samuel Clark, situated three miles southeast of Stony Point, in Jackson County. He had spent the night there and was waiting for breakfast the next morning when Captain Peabody, at the head of one hundred Federal cavalry, surprised the Guerrillas and came on at the charge, shooting and yelling. Instantly dividing the detachment in order that the position might be effectively held, Quantrell, with nine men, took the dwelling, and Gregg, with eight, occupied the smoke house. For a while the fighting was at long range, Peabody holding tenaciously to the timber in front of Clark's, distant about one hundred yards, and refusing to come out. Presently, however, he did an unsoldierly thing—or rather an unskillful thing—he mounted his men and forced them to charge the dwelling on horseback. Quantrell's detachment reserved fire until the foremost horseman was within thirty feet, and Gregg permitted those operating against his position, to come even closer. Then, a quick, sure volley, and twenty-seven men and horses went down together. Badly demoralized, but in no manner defeated, Peabody rallied again in the timber, while Quantrell, breaking out from the dwelling house and gathering up Gregg as he went, charged the Federals fiercely in return and with something of success. The impetus of the rush carried him past a portion of the Federal line, where some of their horses were hitched, and the return of the wave brought with it nine valuable animals. It was over the horses that Andrew Blunt had a hand-to-hand fight with a splendid Federal trooper. Both were very brave.

Blunt had just joined. No one knew his history. He asked no questions and he answered none. Some said he had once belonged to the cavalry of the regular army; others, that behind the terrible record of the Guerrillas he wished to find isolation. Singling out a fine sorrel horse from among the number fastened in his front, Blunt was just about to unhitch him when a Federal trooper, superbly mounted, dashed down to the line and fired and missed. Blunt left his position by the side of the horse and strode out into the open, accepting the challenge defiantly, and closed with his antagonist. The first time he fired he missed, although many men believed him a better shot than Quantrell. The Federal sat on his horse calmly and fired the second shot deliberately and again missed. Blunt went four paces toward him, took a quick aim and fired very much as a man would at something running. Out of the Federal's blue overcoat a little jet of dust spurted up and he reeled in his seat. The man, hit hard in the breast, did not fall, however. He gripped his saddle with his knees, cavalry fashion, steadied himself in his stirrups and fired three times at Blunt in quick succession. They were now but twenty paces apart, and the Guerrilla was shortening the distance. When at ten he fired his third shot. The heavy dragoon ball struck the gallant Federal fair in the forehead and knocked him dead from his horse.

While the duel was in progress, brief as it was, Blunt had not watched his rear, to gain which a dozen Federals had started from the extreme right. He saw them, but he did not hurry. Going back to the coveted steed, he mounted him deliberately and dashed back through the lines closed up behind him, getting a fierce hurrah of encouragement from his own comrades, and a wicked volley from the enemy.

It was time. A second company of Federals in the neighborhood, attracted by the firing, had made a junction with Peabody and were already closing in upon the houses from the south. Surrounded now by one hundred and sixty men, Quantrell was in almost the same straits as at the Tate house. His horses were in the hands of the Federals, it was some little distance to the timber, and the environment was complete. Captain Peabody, himself a Kansas man, knew who led the forces opposed to him and burned with a desire to make a finish of this Quantrell and his reckless band at one fell sweep. Not content with the one hundred and sixty men already in positions about the house, he sent off posthaste to Pink Hill for additional reinforcements. Emboldened also by their numbers, the Federals had approached so close to the positions held by the Guerrillas that it was possible for them to utilize the shelter the fences gave. Behind these they ensconced themselves while pouring a merciless fusillade upon the dwelling house and smoke house in comparative immunity. This annoyed Quantrell, distressed Gregg and made Cole Younger—one of the coolest heads in council ever consulted—look a little anxious. Finally a solution was found. Quantrell would draw the fire of this ambuscade; he would make the concealed enemy show himself. Ordering all to be ready and to fire the very moment the opportunity for execution was best, he dashed out from the dwelling house to the smoke house, and from the smoke house back again to the dwelling house. Eager to kill the daring man, and excited somewhat by their own efforts made to do it, the Federals exposed themselves recklessly. Then, owing to the short range, the revolvers of the Guerrillas began to tell with deadly effect. Twenty at least were shot down along the fences, and as many more wounded and disabled. It was thirty steps from one house to the other, yet Quantrell made the venture eight different times, not less than one hundred men firing at him as he came and went. On his garments there was not even the smell of fire. His life seemed to be charmed—his person protected by some superior presence. When at last even this artifice would no longer enable his men to fight with any degree of equality, Quantrell determined to abandon the houses and the horses and make a dash as of old to the nearest timber. "I had rather lose a thousand horses," he said, when some one remonstrated with him, "than a single man like those who have fought with me this day. Heroes are scarce; horses are everywhere."

In the swift rush that came now, fortune again favored him. Almost every revolver belonging to the Federals was empty. They had been relying altogether upon their carbines in the fight. After the first onset on horseback—one in which the revolvers were principally used—they had failed to reload, and had nothing but empty guns in their hands after Quantrell for the last time drew their fire and dashed away on the heels of it into the timber. Pursuit was not attempted. Enraged at the escape of the Guerrillas, and burdened with a number of dead and wounded altogether out of proportion to the forces engaged, Captain Peabody caused to be burned everything upon the premises which had a plank or shingle about it.

Something else was yet to be done. Getting out afoot as best he could, Quantrell saw a company of cavalry making haste from toward Pink Hill. It was but a short distance to where the road he was skirting crossed a creek, and commanding this crossing was a perpendicular bluff inaccessible to horsemen. Thither he hurried. The work of ambushment was the work of a moment. George Todd, alone of all the Guerrillas, had brought with him from the house a shotgun. In running for life, the most of them were unencumbered. The approaching Federals were the reinforcements Peabody had ordered up from Pink Hill, and as Quantrell's defense had lasted one hour and a half, they were well on their way.

As they came to the creek, the foremost riders halted that their horses might drink. Soon others crowded in until all the ford was thick with animals. Just then from the bluff above a leaden rain fell as hail might from a cloudless sky. Rearing steeds trampled upon wounded riders; the dead dyed the clear water red. Wild panic laid hold of the helpless mass, cut into gaps, and flight beyond the range of the deadly revolvers came first of all and uppermost. There was a rally, however. Once out from under the fire the lieutenant commanding the detachment called a halt. He was full of dash, and meant to see more of the unknown on the top of the hill. Dismounting his men and putting himself at their head, he turned back for a fight, marching resolutely forward to the bluff. Quantrell waited for the attack to develop itself. The lieutenant moved right onward. When within fifty paces of the position, George Todd rose up from behind a rock and covered the young Federal with his unerring shotgun. It seemed a pity to kill him, he was so brave and collected, and yet he fell riddled just as he had drawn his sword and shouted "Forward!" to the lagging men. At Todd's signal there succeeded a fierce revolver volley, and again were the Federals driven from the hills and back towards their horses.

Satisfied with the results of this fight—made solely as a matter of revenge for burning Clark's buildings—Quantrell fell away from the ford and continued his retreat on towards his rendezvous upon the waters of the Sni. Peabody, however, had not had his way. Coming on himself in the direction of Pink Hill, and mistaking these reinforcements for Guerrillas, he had quite a lively fight with them, each detachment getting in several volleys and killing and wounding a goodly number before either discovered the mistake.

"The only prisoner I ever shot during the war," relates Captain Trow, "was a 'nigger' I captured on guard at Independence, Missouri, who claimed that he had killed his master and burned his houses and barns. The circumstances were these: Captain Blunt and I one night went to town for a little spree and put on our Federal uniforms. While there we came in contact with the camp guard, which was a 'nigger' and a white man. They did not hear us until we got right up to them, so we, claiming to be Federals, arrested them for not doing their duty in hailing us at a distance. We took them prisoners, disarmed them, took them down to the Fire Prairie bottom east of Independence about ten miles, and there I thought I would have to kill the 'nigger' on account of his killing his master and burning his property. I shot him in the forehead just above the eyes. I even put my finger in the bullet hole to be sure I had him. The ball never entered his skull, but went round it. To make sure of him, I shot him in the foot and he never flinched, so I left him for dead. He came to, however, that night and crawled out into the road, and a man from Independence came along the next morning and took him in his wagon. This I learned several years afterwards at Independence in a saloon when one day I chanced to be taking a drink. There I met the 'nigger' whom I thought dead. He recognized me from hearing my name spoken and asked if I remembered shooting a 'nigger.' I said 'Yes.' I had the pleasure of taking a drink with him."

JAYHAWKERS AND MILITIA MURDER OLD MAN BLYTHE'S SON

QUANTRELL and His Company Were on Foot Again and Jackson County was filled with troops. At Kansas City there was a large garrison, with smaller ones at Independence, Pink Hill, Lone Jack, Stoney Point and Sibley. Peabody caused the report to be circulated that a majority of Quantrell's men were wounded, and that if the brush were scoured thoroughly they might be picked up here and there and summarily disposed of. Raiding bands therefore began the hunt. Old men were imprisoned because they could give no information of a concealed enemy; young men murdered outright; women were insulted and abused. The uneasiness that had heretofore rested upon the county gave place now to a feeling of positive fear. The Jayhawkers on one side and the militia on the other made matters hot. All traveling was dangerous. People at night closed their eyes in dread lest the morrow should usher in a terrible awakening. One incident of the hunt is a bloody memory yet with many of the older settlers of Jackson County.

An aged man by the name of Blythe, believing his own house to be his own, fed all whom he pleased to feed, and sheltered all whom it pleased him to shelter. Among many of his warm personal friends was Cole Younger. The colonel commanding the fort at Independence sent a scout one day to find Younger, and to make the country people tell where he might be found. Old man Blythe was not at home, but his son was, a fearless lad of twelve years. He was taken to the barn and ordered to confess everything he knew of Quantrell, Younger, and their whereabouts. If he failed to speak truly he was to be killed. The boy, in no manner frightened, kept them some moments in conversation, waiting for an opportunity to escape. Seeing at last what he imagined to be a chance, he dashed away from his captors and entered the house under a perfect shower of balls. There, seizing a pistol and rushing through the back door towards some timber, a ball struck him in the spine just as he reached the garden fence and he fell back dying, but splendid in his boyish courage to the last. Turning over on his face as the Jayhawkers rushed up to finish him he shot one dead, mortally wounded another, and severely wounded the third. Before he could shoot a fourth time, seventeen bullets were put into his body.

It seemed as if God's vengeance was especially exercised in the righting of this terrible wrong. An old negro man who had happened to be at Blythe's house at the time, was a witness to the bloody deed, and, afraid of his own life, ran hurriedly into the brush. There he came unawares upon Younger, Quantrell, Haller, Todd, and eleven of his men. Noticing the great excitement under which the negro labored, they forced him to tell them the whole story. It was yet time for an ambuscade. On the road back to Independence was a pass between two embankments known as "The Blue Cut." In width it was about fifty yards, and the height of each embankment was about thirty feet. Quantrell dismounted his men, stationed some at each end of the passageway and some at the top on either side. Not a shot was to be fired until the returning Federals had entered it, front and rear. From the Blue Cut this fatal spot was afterwards known as the Slaughter Pen. Of the thirty-eight Federals sent out after Cole Younger, and who, because they could not find him, had brutally murdered an innocent boy, seventeen were killed while five—not too badly shot to be able to ride—barely managed to escape into Independence, the avenging Guerrillas hard upon their heels.

THE LOW HOUSE FIGHT

THE next rendezvous was at Reuben Harris', ten miles south of Independence, and thither all the command went, splendidly mounted again and eager for employment. Some days of preparation were necessary. Richard Hall, a fighting blacksmith, who shot as well as he shod, and knew a trail as thoroughly as a piece of steel, had need to exercise much of his handiwork in order to make the horses good for cavalry. Then there were several rounds of cartridges to make. A Guerrilla knew nothing whatever of an ordnance master. His laboratory was in his luck. If a capture did not bring him caps, he had to fall back on ruse, or strategem, or blockade-running square out. Powder and lead in the raw were enough, for if with these he could not make himself presentable at inspection he had no calling as a fighter in the brush.

It was Quantrell's intention at this time to attack Harrisonville, the county seat of Cass County, and capture it if possible. With this object in view, and after every preparation was made for a vigorous campaign, he moved eight miles east of Independence, camping near the Little Blue, in the vicinity of Job Crabtree's. He camped always near or in a house. For this he had two reasons. First, that its occupants might gather up for him all the news possible; and, second, that in the event of a surprise a sure rallying point would always be at hand. He had a theory that after a Guerrilla was given time to get over the first effects of a sudden charge or ambushment the very nature of his military status made him invincible; that after an opportunity was afforded him to think, a surrender was next to impossible.

Before there was time to attack Harrisonville, however, a scout reported Peabody again on the war path, this time bent on an utter extermination of the Guerrillas, and he well-nigh kept his word. From Job Crabtree's, Quantrell had moved to an unoccupied house known as the Low house, and then from this house he had gone to some contiguous timber to bivouac for the night. About ten o'clock the sky suddenly became overcast, a fresh wind blew from the east, and rain fell in torrents. Again the house was occupied, the horses being hitched along the fence in the rear of it, the door on the south, the only door, having a bar across it in lieu of a sentinel. Such soldiering was perfectly inexcusable, and it taught Quantrell a lesson to remember until the day of his death.

In the morning preceding the day of the attack Lieutenant Nash, of Peabody's regiment, commanding two hundred men, had struck Quantrell's trail, but lost it later on, and then found it again just about sunset. He was informed of Quantrell's having gone from the Low house to the brush and of his having come back to it when the rain began falling heavily. To a certain extent this seeking shelter was a necessity on the part of Quantrell. The men had no cartridge boxes, and not all of them had overcoats. If once their ammunition were damaged, it would be as though sheep should attack wolves.

Nash, supplied with everything needed for the weather, waited patiently for the Guerrillas to become snugly settled under shelter, and then surrounded the house. Before a gun was fired the Federals had every horse belonging to the Guerrillas, and were bringing to bear every available carbine in command upon the only door. At first all was confusion. Across the logs that once had supported an upper floor some boards had been laid, and sleeping upon them were Todd, Blunt and William Carr. Favored by the almost impenetrable darkness, Quantrell determined upon an immediate abandonment of the house. He called loudly twice for all to follow him and dashed through the door under a galling fire. Those in the loft did not hear him, and maintained in reply to the Federal volleys a lively fusillade. Then Cole Younger, James Little, Joseph Gilchrist and a young Irish boy—a brave new recruit—turned back to help their comrades. The house became a furnace. At each of the two corners on the south side four men fought, Younger calling on Todd in the intervals of every volley to come out of the loft and come to the brush. They started at last. It was four hundred yards to the nearest shelter, and the ground was very muddy. Gilchrist was shot down, the Irish boy was killed, Blunt was wounded and captured, Carr surrendered, Younger had his hat shot away, Little was unhurt, and Todd, scratched in four places, finally got safely to the timber. But it was a miracle. Twenty Federals singled him out as well as they could in the darkness and kept close at his heels, firing whenever a gun was loaded. Todd had a musket which, when it seemed as if they were all upon him at once, he would point at the nearest and make pretense of shooting. When they halted and dodged about to get out of range, he would dash away again, gaining what space he could until he had to turn and re-enact the same unpleasant pantomime. Reaching the woods at last, he fired point blank, and in reality now, killing with a single discharge one pursuer and wounding four. Part of Nash's command were still on the track of Quantrell, but after losing five killed and a number wounded, they returned again to the house, but returned too late for the continued battle. The dead and two prisoners were all that were left for them.

Little Blue was bank full and the country was swarming with militia. For the third time Quantrell was afoot with unrelenting pursuers upon his trail in every direction. At daylight Nash would be after him again, river or no river. He must get over or fare worse. The rain was still pouring down; muddy, forlorn, well-nigh worn out, yet in no manner demoralized, just as Quantrell reached the Little Blue he saw on the other bank Toler, one of his own soldiers, sitting in a canoe. Thence forward the work of crossing was easy, and Nash, coming on an hour afterwards, received a volley at the ford where he expected to find a lot of helpless and unresisting men.

This fight at the Low house occurred the first week in May, 1862, and caused the expedition against Harrisonville to be abandoned. Three times surprised and three times losing all horses, saddles, and bridles, it again became necessary to disband the Guerrillas in this instance as in the preceding two. The men were dismissed for thirty days with orders to remount themselves, while Quantrell—taking Todd into his confidence and acquainting him fully with his plans—started in his company for Hannibal. It had become urgently necessary to replenish the supply of revolver caps. The usual trade with Kansas City was cut off. Of late the captures had not been as plentiful as formerly. Recruits were coming in, and the season for larger operations was at hand. In exploits where peril and excitement were about evenly divided, Quantrell took great delight. He was so cool, so calm; he had played before such a deadly game; he knew so well how to smile when a smile would win, and when to frown when a frown was a better card to play, that something in this expedition appealed to every quixotic instinct of his intrepidity. Todd was all iron; Quantrell all glue. Todd would go at a circular saw; Quantrell would sharpen its teeth and grease it where there was friction. One purred and killed, and the other roared and killed. What mattered the mode, however, only so the end was the same?

QUANTRELL AND TODD GO AFTER AMMUNITION

CLAD in the full uniform of Federal majors—a supply of which Quantrell kept always on hand, even in a day so early in the war as this—Quantrell and Todd rode into Hamilton, a little town on the Hannibal & St. Louis Railroad, and remained for the night at the principal hotel. A Federal garrison was there—two companies of Iowa infantry—and the captain commanding took a great fancy to Todd, insisting that he should leave the hotel for his quarters and share his blankets with him.

Two days were spent in Hannibal, where an entire Feneral regiment was stationed. Here Quantrell was more circumspect. When asked to give an account of himself and his companion, he replied promptly that Todd was a major of the Sixth Missouri Cavalry and himself the major of the Ninth. Unacquainted with either organization, the commander at Hannibal had no reason to believe otherwise. Then he asked about that special cut-throat Quantrell. Was it true that he fought under a black flag? Had he ever really belonged to the Jayhawkers? How much truth was there in the stories of the newspapers about his operations and prowess? Quantrell became voluble. In rapid yet picturesque language he painted a perfect picture of the war along the border. He told of Todd, Jarrette, Blunt, Younger, Haller, Poole, Shepherd, Gregg, Little, the Cogers, and all of his best men just as they were, and himself also just as he was, and closed the conversation emphatically by remarking: "If you were here, Colonel, surrounded as you are by a thousand soldiers, and they wanted you, they would come and get you."

From Hannibal—after buying quietly and at various times and in various places fifty thousand revolver caps—Quantrell and Todd went boldly into St. Joseph. This city was full of soldiers. Colonel Harrison B. Branch was there in command of a regiment of militia—a brave, conservative, right-thinking soldier—and Quantrell introduced himself to Branch as Major Henderson of the Sixth Missouri. Todd, by this time, had put on, in lieu of a major's epaulettes, with its distinguishing leaf, the barred ones of a captain. "Too many majors traveling together," quaintly remarked Todd, "are like too many roses in a boquet: the other flowers don't have a chance. Let me be a captain for the balance of the trip."

Colonel Branch made himself very agreeable to Major Henderson and Captain Gordon, and asked Todd if he were a relative of the somewhat notorious Si Gordon of Platte, relating at the same time an interesting adventure he once had with him. En route from St. Louis, in 1861, to the headquarters of his regiment, Colonel Branch, with one hundred and thirty thousand dollars on his person, found that he would have to remain in Weston over night and the better part of the next day. Before he got out of the town Gordon took it, and with it he took Colonel Branch. Many of Gordon's men were known to him, and it was eminently to his interest just then to renew old acquaintanceship and be extremely complaisant to the new. Wherever he could find the largest number of Guerrillas there he was among them, calling for whiskey every now and then, incessantly telling some agreeable story or amusing anecdote. Thus he got through with what seemed to him an interminably long day. Not a dollar of his money was touched, Gordon releasing him unconditionally when the town was abandoned and bidding him make haste to get out lest the next lot of raiders made it the worse for him.

For three days, off and on, Quantrell was either with Branch at his quarters or in company with him about town. Todd, elsewhere and indefatigable, was rapidly buying caps and revolvers. Branch introduced Quantrell to General Ben Loan, discussed Penick with him and Penick's regiment—a St. Joseph officer destined in the near future to give Quantrell some stubborn fighting—passed in review the military situation, incidently referred to the Guerrillas of Jackson County and the savage nature of the warfare going on there, predicted the absolute destruction of African slavery, and assisted Quantrell in many ways in making his mission thoroughly successful. For the first and last time in his life Colonel Branch was disloyal to the government and the flag—he gave undoubted aid and encouragement during those three days to about as uncompromising an enemy as either ever had.

From St. Joseph Quantrell and Todd came to Kansas City in a hired hack, first sending into Jackson County a man unquestionably devoted to the South with the whole amount of purchases made in both Hannibal and St. Joseph.

A CHALLENGE

QUANTRELL with his band of sixty-three men were being followed by a force of seven hundred cavalrymen under Peabody. Peabody came up in the advance with three hundred men, while four hundred marched at a supporting distance behind him. Quantrell halted at Swearington's barn and the Guerrillas were drying their blankets. One picket, Hick George, an iron man, who could sleep in his saddle and eat as he ran and who suspected every act until he could fathom it, watched the rear against an attack. Peabody received George's fire, for George would fire at an angel or devil in the line of his duty, and drove him toward Quantrell at a full run. Every preparation possible under the circumstances had been made and if the reception was not as cordial as expected, the Federals could attribute it to the long march and the rainy weather.

Quantrell stood at the gate calmly with his hand on the latch; when George entered he would close and fasten it. Peabody's forces were within thirty feet of the fence when the Guerrillas delivered a crashing blow and sixteen Federals crashed against the barricade and fell there. Others fell and more dropped out here and there before the disorganized mass got back safe again from the deadly revolver range. After them Quantrell himself dashed hotly, George Maddox, Jarrette, Cole Younger, George Morrow, Gregg, Blunt, Poole and Haller following them fast to the timber and upon their return gathering all the arms and ammunition of the killed as they went. At the timber Peabody rearranged his lines, dismounted his men and came forward again at a quick run, yelling. Do what he would, the charge spent itself before it could be called a charge.

Peabody arranged his men, dismounted them, and came forward again at a double-quick, and yelling. Do what he would, the charge again spent itself before it could be called a charge. Never nearer than one hundred yards of the fence, he skirmished at long range for nearly an hour and finally took up a position one mile south of the barn, awaiting reinforcements. Quantrell sent out Cole Younger, Poole, John Brinker and William Haller to "lay up close to Peabody," as he expressed it, and keep him and his movements steadily in view.

The four daredevils multiplied themselves. They attacked the pickets, rode around the whole camp in bravado, firing upon it from every side, and finally agreed to send a flag of truce in to Peabody with this manner of a challenge:

"We, whose names are hereunto affixed, respectfully ask of Colonel Peabody the privilege of fighting eight of his best men, hand to hand, and that he himself make the selection and send them out to us immediately."

This was signed by the following: Coleman Younger, William Haller, David

Poole and John Brinker.

Younger bore it. Tieing a white handkerchief to a stick he rode boldly up to the nearest picket and asked for a parley. Six started towards him and he bade four go back. The message was carried to Peabody, but he laughed at it and scanned the prairie in every direction for the coming reinforcements. Meanwhile Quantrell was retreating. His four men cavorting about Peabody were to amuse him as long as possible and then get away as best they could. Such risks are often taken in war; to save one thousand men, one hundred are sometimes sacrificed. Death equally with exactness has its mathematics.

The reinforcements came up rapidly. One hundred joined Peabody on the prairie, and two hundred masked themselves by some timber on the north and advanced parallel with Quantrell's line of retreat—a flank movement meant to be final. Haller hurried off to Quantrell to report, and Peabody, vigorous and alert, now threw out a cloud of cavalry skirmishers after the three remaining Guerrillas. The race was one for life. Both started their horses on a keen run. It was on the eve of harvest, and the wheat, breast high to the horse, flew away from before the feet of the racers as though the wind were driving through it an incarnate scythe blade. As Poole struck the eastern edge of this wheat a very large jack, belonging to Swearingen, joined in the pursuit, braying loudly at every jump, and leading the Federals by a length. Comedy and tragedy were in the same field together. Carbines rang out, revolvers cracked, the jack brayed, the Federals roared with merriment, and looking back over his shoulder as he rode on, Poole heard the laughter and saw the jack, and imagined the devil to be after him leading a lot of crazy people.

THE BATTLE AND CAPTURE OF INDEPENDENCE

"ON August 11, 1862," says Trow, "about a month prior to the capture of Independence, while Press Webb and I were out on a little frolic, we attended a dance at his father's, Ace Webb, and stayed all night there. During the night a regiment of soldiers surrounded the house. We barred the doors against them and I aimed to get away in a woman's garb and had my dress all on, bonnet and everything, with permission to get out of the house with the women without being fired upon. But old Mrs. Webb objected to my going out for fear it would cause her son to be killed, so I had to pull off the dress and hide my pistols in the straw tick under the feather bed and surrender to them. I was taken to Independence and made a prisoner for a month.

"While in prison several incidents happened. A Federal officer in the prison who called himself Beauregard, was put into jail with me for some misdemeanor and challenged me to a sparring match, with the understanding that neither one of us was to strike the other in the face. However, he hit me in the face the first thing he did and I kicked him in the stomach and kept on kicking him until I kicked him down the stairs. For this offense I was chained down on my back for ten hours.

"The provost marshal would come in once in a while and entertain me while I was chained down. He was a Dutchman, and would say in broken Dutch, 'How duse youse like it?' and would sing me a song something like this: 'Don't youse vish you vas in Dixie, you d— —d old secess?' and dance around me.

"After I had been there a few days they cleaned up the prison and took out the rubbage and dirt. Press Webb, who had been captured with me, and I were detailed to do the work. We had an understanding that when we went out into the back yard, which was walled, we were each to capture the guards who were guarding us, take their arms and scale the wall. But Webb weakened and would not attempt to take his man, so we did not attempt to get away then. Then I was court-martialed and remained there in jail, while Webb was sent to Alton prison. I was held there under court-martial and sentenced to be shot.

"All this time Quantrell was trying to hear from me, whether I had been killed, and at the same time getting the boys together to make a raid on Independence and try to capture the town and release me from jail, all unbeknown to me, should I still be alive. Colonel Hughes had joined Quantrell with his company, the expedition being agreed between Quantrell and Colonel Hughes. Colonel Hughes asked Quantrell for some accurate information touching the strongest and best fortified points about the town. It was three days previous to the attack; the day before it was begun the information should be forthcoming. 'Leave it to me,' said Cole Younger, when the promise made to Hughes had been repeated by Quantrell, 'and when you report you can report the facts. A soldier wants nothing else.' The two men separated. It was the 7th day of August, 1862.

"On the 8th, at about ten o'clock in the morning, an old woman with gray hair and wearing spectacles, rode up to the public square from the south. Independence was alive with soldiers; several market wagons were about the streets—the trade in vegetables and the traffic in fruit were lively. This old woman was one of the ancient time. A faded sunbonnet, long and antique, hid almost all her face. The riding skirt, which once had been black, was now bleached; some tatters also abounded, and here and there an unsightly patch. On the horse was a blind bridle, the left rein leather and the right one a rope. Neither did it have a throat latch. The saddle was a man's saddle, strong in the stirrups and fit for any service. Women resorted often to such saddles then; Civil War had made many a hard thing easy. On the old lady's arm was a huge market basket, covered by a white cloth. Under the cloth were beets, garden beans and some summer apples. As she passed the first picket he jibed at her. 'Good morning, grandmother,' he said. 'Does the rebel crop need any rain out in your country?' Where the reserve post was the sergeant on duty took her horse by the bridle, and peered up under her bonnet and into her face. 'Were you younger and prettier I might kiss you,' he said. 'Were I younger and prettier,' the old lady said, 'I might box your ears for your impudence.'

"'Oh, ho! you old she-wolf, what claws you have for scratching,' and the rude soldier took her hand with an oath and looked at it sneeringly. She drew it away with a quick motion and started her horse so rapidly ahead that he did not have time to examine it. In a moment he was probably ashamed of himself, and so let her ride on uninterrupted.

"Once well in town no one noticed her any more. At the camp she was seen to stop and give three soldiers some apples out of her basket. The sentinel in front of Buell's headquarters was overheard to say to a comrade: 'There's the making of four good bushwhacking horses yet in that old woman's horse,' and two hours later, as she rode back past the reserve picket post, the sergeant still on duty, did not halt her himself, but caused one of his guards to do it; he was anxious to know what the basket contained, for in many ways of late arms and ammunition had been smuggled out to the enemy.

"At first the old lady did not heed the summons to halt—that short, rasping, ominous call which in all tongues appears to have the same sound; she did, however, shift the basket from the right arm to the left and straighten up in the saddle for the least appreciable bit. Another cry and the old lady looked back innocently over one shoulder and snapped out: 'Do you mean me?' By this time a mounted picket had galloped up to her, ranged alongside and seized the bridle of the horse. It was thirty steps back to the post, maybe, where the sergeant and eight men were down from their horses and the horses hitched. To the outpost it was a hundred yards, and a single picket stood there. The old woman said to the soldier, as he was turning her horse around and doing it roughly: 'What will you have? I'm but a poor lone woman going peacefully to my home.' 'Didn't you hear the sergeant call for you, d— —n you? Do you want to be carried back?' the sentinel made answer.

"The face under the sunbonnet transformed itself; the demure eyes behind their glasses grew scintillant. From beneath the riding skirt a heavy foot emerged; the old horse in the blind bridle seemed to undergo an electric impulse; there was the gliding of the old hand which the sergeant had inspected into the basket, and a cocked pistol came out and was fired almost before it got in sight. With his grasp still upon the reins of the old woman's bridle, the Federal picket fell dead under the feet of the horse. Then stupified, the impotent reserve saw a weird figure dash away down the road, its huge bonnet flapping in the wind, and the trail of an antique riding skirt, split at the shoulders, streaming back as the smoke that follows a furnace. Coleman Younger had accomplished his mission. Beneath the bonnet and the bombazine was the Guerrilla, and beneath the white cloth of the basket and its apples and beets and beans the unerring revolvers. The furthest picket heard the firing, saw the apparition, bethought himself of the devil, and took to the brush.

"During this month's stay in prison, being chained down, drinking coffee sweet as molasses, when they knew I did not like sweetened coffee they made it that much sweeter, running a boxing match, having songs sung to me of the sweet South in an insulting way and being janitor for the jail and thousands of other things that go with a prison life, and while Cole Younger was getting information under disguise as an old lady Sally selling apples and cookies to the Federals three days before, I made my bond, my father being a Union man and interceding with Colonel Buell in my behalf. I made bond for $50,000 to report at headquarters every two hours during the day and be locked up at night.

"About the third day after I gave bond and after I was thoroughly acquainted with the location of the soldiers I made my escape through the back way, through the guard, and found my way to a near-by friend by the name of Sullivan and got a horse and saddle, went by Webb's and got my pistols out of a hollow log back of the barn where Mrs. Webb had hid them, and rode on to Quantrell's camp, arriving there about eleven o'clock that night. After telling Quantrell how the soldiers and camps were located, and as Younger had told him about six hours before, it was decided to make the charge the next morning, and after a hard night's riding we struck Independence just a little before daylight on the morning of August 11, 1862, surprised the camp, and nine hundred soldiers, with the exception of the colonel, who was in command, surrendered to two hundred and fifty of us. Colonel Buell was quartered in a brick building with his body guard and it was not until about nine o'clock that he surrendered. Buell lost about three hundred killed, besides three hundred and seventy-five wounded. We had a loss of only one man killed and four wounded. In attempting to take the provost marshal, who tortured me so when I was in prison, Kitt Child was shot and killed, making two men lost in the attack, all told.

"In the skirmish I was badly cut up by a saber, but I got away from them on foot, and so did Quantrell. While the colonel was slashing at me I struck him with a heavy dragoon pistol and burst his knee cap and he fell off his horse. This ended the fight. That night we got together at camp and Quantrell came in on foot, and I had to remount.

"If Quantrell's men could have been decorated for that day's fight, and if at review some typical thing that stood for glory could have passed along the ranks, calling the roll of the brave, there would have answered modestly, yet righteously, Trow, Haller, Gregg, Jarrette, Morris, Poole, Younger, James Tucker, Blunt, George Shepherd, Yager, Hicks, George, Sim Whitsett, Fletch Taylor, John Ross, Dick Burns, Kit Chiles, Dick Maddox, Fernando Scott, Sam Clifton, George Maddox, Sam Hamilton, Press Webb, John Coger, Dan Vaughn, and twenty others, some dead now, but dead in vain for their country. There were no decorations, however, but there was a deliverance. Crammed in the county jail, and sweltering in the midsummer's heat, were old men who had been pioneers in the land, and young men who had been sentenced to die. The first preached the Confederacy and it triumphant; the last to make it so, enlisted for the war. These jailbirds, either as missionaries or militants, had work to do."

THE LONE JACK FIGHT

ONCE there stood a lone blackjack tree, taller than its companions and larger than any near it. From this tree the town of Lone Jack, in the eastern portion of Jackson County, was named. On the afternoon of the 13th of August clouds were seen gathering there. These clouds were cavalrymen. Succoring recruits in every manner possible, and helping them on to rendezvous by roads, or lanes, or water courses, horsemen acquainted with the country kept riding continuously up and down. A company of these on the evening of the 15th were in the village of Lone Jack.

Major Emory L. Foster, doing active scouting duty in the region round about Lexington, had his headquarters in the town. The capture of Independence had been like a blow upon the cheek; he would avenge it. He knew how to fight. There was dash about him; he had enterprise. Prairie life had enlarged his vision and he did not see the war like a martinet; he felt within him the glow of generous ambition; he loved his uniform for the honor it had; he would see about that Independence business—about that Quantrell living there between the two Blues and raiding the West—about those gray recruiting folks riding up from the South—about the tales of ambuscades that were told eternally of Jackson County, and of all the toils spread for the unwary Jayhawkers. He had heard, too, of the company which halted a moment in Lone Jack as it passed through, and of course it was Quantrell.

It was six o'clock when the Confederates were there, and eight o'clock when the Federal colonel, Colonel Foster, marched in, leading nine hundred and eighty-five cavalrymen, with two pieces of Rabb's Indiana battery—a battery much celebrated for tenacious gunners and accurate firing. Cockrell, who was in command, knew Foster well; the other Confederates knew nothing of him. He was there, however, and that was positive proof enough that he wanted to fight. Seven hundred Confederates—armed with shotguns, horse pistols, squirrel rifles, regulation guns, and what not—attacked nine hundred and eighty-five Federal cavalrymen in a town for a position, and armed with Spencer rifles and Colt's revolvers, dragoon size. There was also the artillery. Lone Jack sat quietly in the green of emerald prairie, its orchards in fruit and its harvests goodly. On the west was timber, and in this timber a stream ran musically along. To the east the prairies stretched, their glass waves crested with sunshine. On the north there were groves in which birds abounded. In some even the murmuring of doves was heard, and an infinite tremor ran over all the leaves as the wind stirred the languid pulse of summer into fervor.

COLE YOUNGER GOING TO INDEPENDENCE

In the center of the town a large hotel made a strong fortification. The house from being a tavern, had come to be a redoubt. From the top the Stars and Stripes floated proudly—a tricolor that had upon it then more of sunshine than of blood. Later the three colors had become as four.

On the verge of the prairie nearest the town a hedge row stood as a line of infantry dressed for battle. It was plumed on the sides with tawny grass. The morning broke upon it and upon armed men crouching there, with a strange barred banner and with guns at trail. Here they waited, eager for the signal.

Joining Hays on the left was Cockrell and the detachments of Hays, Rathburn and Bohannon. Their arms were as varied as their uniforms. It was a duel they were going into and each man had the gun he could best handle. From the hedgerow, from the green growing corn, from the orchards and the groves, soldiers could not see much save the flag flying skyward on the redoubt on the Cave House.

At five o'clock a solitary gunshot aroused camp and garrison, and all the soldiers stood face to face with imminent death. No one knew thereafter how the fight commenced. It was Missourian against Missourian—neighbor against neighbor—the rival flags waved over each and the killing went on. This battle had about it a strange fascination. The combatants were not numerous, yet they fought as men seldom fight in detached bodies. The same fury extended to an army would have ended in annihilation. A tree was a fortification. A hillock was an ambush. The cornfields, from being green, became lurid. Dead men were in the groves. The cries of the wounded came in from the apple orchards. All the houses in the town were garrisoned. It was daylight upon the prairies, yet there were lights in the windows—the light of musket flashes.

There is not much to say about the fight in the way of description. The Federals were in Lone Jack; the Confederates had to get them out. House fighting and street fighting are always desperate. The hotel became a hospital, later a holocaust, and over all rose and shone a blessed sun while the airy fingers of the breeze ruffled the oak leaves and tuned the swaying branches to the sound of a psalm.

The graycoats crept nearer. On east, west, north or south. Hays, Cockrell, Tracy, Jackman, Rathburn or Hunter gained ground. Farmer lads in their first battle began gawkies and ended grenadiers. Old plug hats rose and fell as the red fight ebbed and flowed; the shotgun's heavy boom made clearer still the rifle's sharp crack. An hour passed, the struggle had lasted since daylight.

Foster fought his men splendidly. Wounded once, he did not make complaint; wounded again, he kept his place; wounded a third time he stood with his men until courage and endurance only prolonged a sacrifice. Once Haller, commanding thirty of Quantrell's old men, swept up to the guns and over them, the play of their revolvers being as the play of the lightning in a summer cloud. He could not hold them, brave as he was. Then Jackman rushed at them again and bore them backward twenty paces or more. Counter-charged, they hammered his grip loose and drove him down the hill. Then Hays and Hunter—with the old plug hats and wheezy rifles—finished the throttling; the lions were done roaring.

Tracy had been wounded. Hunter wounded. Hays wounded, Captains Bryant and Bradley killed, among the Confederates, together with thirty-six others and one hundred and thirty-four wounded. Among the Federals, Foster, the commander, was nigh unto death; his brother, Captain Foster, mortally shot, died afterwards. One hundred and thirty-six dead lay about the streets and houses of the town, and five hundred and fifty wounded made up the aggregate of a fight, numbers considered, as desperate and bloody as any that ever crimsoned the annals of a civil war. A few more than two hundred breaking through the Confederate lines on the south, where they were weakest, rushed furiously into Lexington, Haller in pursuit as some beast of prey, leaping upon everything which attempted to make a stand between Lone Jack and Wellington. Captain Trow, who was in this battle, narrates that at one time during the battle, "I was forced to lie down and roll across the street to save my scalp."

A mighty blow seemed impending. Commanders turned pale, and lest this head or that head felt the trip-hammer, all the heads kept wagging and dodging. Burris got out of Cass County; Jennison hurried into Kansas; the Guerrillas kept a sort of open house; and the recruits—drove after drove and mostly unarmed—hastened southward. Then the Federal wave, which had at first receded beyond all former boundaries, flowed back again and inundated Western Missouri. Quantrell's nominal battalion, yielding to the exodus, left him only the old guard as a rallying point. It was necessary again to reorganize.

After the Guerrillas had reorganized they stripped themselves for steady fighting. Federal troops were everywhere, infantry at the posts, cavalry on the war paths. The somber defiance mingled with despair did not come until 1864; in 1862 the Guerrillas laughed as they fought. And they fought by streams and bridges, where roads crossed and forked and where trees or hollows were. They fought from houses and hay stacks; on foot and on horseback; at night when the weird laughter of owls could be heard in the thickets; in daylight, when the birds sang as they found sweet rest. The black flag was being woven, but it had not yet been unfurled.

Breaking suddenly out of Jackson County, Quantrell raided Shawneetown, Kansas, and captured its garrison of fifty militia. Then at Olathe, Kansas, the next day, the right hand did what the left one finished so well at Shawneetown; seventy-five Federals surrendered there. Each garrison was patrolled and set free save seven from Shawneetown; these were Jennison's Jayhawkers and they had to die. A military execution is where one man kills another; it is horrible. In battle, one does not see death. He is there, surely—he is in that battery's smoke, on the crest of that hill fringed with the fringe of pallid faces, under the hoofs of the horses, yonder where the blue or the gray line creeps onward trailing ominous guns—but his cold, calm eyes look at no single victim.

The seven men rode into Missouri from Shawneetown puzzled; when the heavy timber along the Big Blue was reached and a halt made, they were praying. Quantrell sat upon his horse looking at the Kansans. His voice was unmoved, his countenance perfectly indifferent as he ordered: "Bring ropes; four on one tree, three on another." All of a sudden death stood in the midst of them, and was recognized. One poor fellow gave a cry as piercing as the neighing of a frightened horse. Two trembled, and trembling is the first step towards kneeling. They had not talked any save among themselves up to this time, but when they saw Blunt busy with some ropes, one spoke up to Quantrell: "Captain, just a word: the pistol before the rope; a soldier's before a dog's death. As for me, I'm ready." Of all the seven this was the youngest—how brave he was.

The prisoners were arranged in line, the Guerrillas opposite to them. They had confessed to belonging to Jennison, but denied the charge of killing and burning. Quantrell hesitated a moment. His blue eyes searched each face from left to right and back again, and then he ordered: "Take six men, Blunt, and do the work. Shoot the young man and hang the balance."

The oldest man there, some white hair was in his beard, prayed audibly. Some embraced. Silence and twilight, as twin ghosts, crept up the river bank together. Blunt made haste, and before Quantrell had ridden far he heard a pistol shot. He did not even look up; it affected him no more than the tapping of a woodpecker. At daylight the next morning a wood-chopper going early to work saw six stark figures swaying in the river breeze. At the foot of another tree was a dead man and in his forehead a bullet hole—the old mark.

"After Quantrell hanged these men, the only time I was ever scared during the war," relates Captain Trow, "I had left camp one night to visit a lady friend of mine, and a company of Federals got after me, and in the chase I took to the woods and it was at the place where Quantrell had hanged these men. My saddle girth broke right there, but I held on to my horse. I thought the devil and all his angels were after me, but I made it to the camp."

QUANTRELL HANGS SIX MEN ON THE SNI

THE MARCH SOUTH IN 1862

WINTER had come and some snow had fallen. There were no longer any leaves; nature had nothing more to do with the ambuscades. Bitter nights, with a foretaste of more bitter nights to follow, reminded Quantrell that it was time to migrate. Most of the wounded men were well again. All the dismounted had found serviceable horses. On October 22, 1862, a quiet muster on the banks of the Little Blue revealed at inspection nearly all the old faces and forms, with a sprinkling here and there of new ones. Quantrell counted them two by two as the Guerrillas dressed in line, and in front rank and rear rank there were just seventy-eight men. On the morrow they were moving southward. That old road running between Harrisonville and Warrensburg was always to the Guerrilas a road of fire, and here again on their march toward Arkansas, and eight miles east of Harrisonville, did Todd in the advance strike a Federal scout of thirty militia cavalrymen. They were Missourians and led by a Lieutenant Satterlee. To say Todd is to say Charge. To associate him with something that will illustrate him is to put torch and powder magazine together. It was the old, old story. On one side a furious rush, on the other panic and imbecile flight. After a four-mile race it ended with this for a score: Todd, killed, six; Boon Schull, five; Fletch Taylor, three; George Shepherd, two; John Coger, one; Sim Whitsett, one; James Little, one; George Maddox, one; total, twenty; wounded, none. Even in leaving, what sinister farewells these Guerrillas were taking!

The second night out Quantrell stopped over beyond Dayton, in Cass County, and ordered a bivouac for the evening. There came to his camp here a good looking man, clad like a citizen, who had business to transact, and who knew how to state it. He was not fat, he was not heavy. He laughed a good deal, and when he laughed he showed a perfect set of faultlessly white teeth. He was young. An aged man is a thinking ruin; this one did not appear to think—he felt and enjoyed. He was tired of dodging about in the brush, he said, and he believed he would fight a little. Here, there and everywhere the Federals had hunted him and shot at him, and he was weary of so much persecution. "Would Quantrell let him become a Guerrilla?" "Your name?" asked the chief. The recruit winced under the abrupt question slightly, and Quantrell saw the start. Attracted by something of novelty in the whole performance, a crowd collected. Quantrell, without looking at the newcomer, appeared yet to be analyzing him. Suddenly he spoke up: "I have seen you before." "Where?" "Nowhere." "Think again. I have seen you in Lawrence, Kansas." The face was a murderer's face now, softened by a woman's blush. There came to it such a look of mingled fear, indignation and cruel eagerness that Gregg, standing next to him and nearest to him, laid his hand on his revolver. "Stop," said Quantrell, motioning to Gregg; "do not harm him, but disarm him." Two revolvers were taken from his person and a pocket pistol—a Derringer. While being searched the white teeth shone in a smile that was almost placid. "You suspect me," he said, so calmly that his words sounded as if spoken under the vault of some echoing dome. "But I have never been in Lawrence in my life."

Quantrell was lost in thought again, with the strange man—standing up smiling in the midst of the band—watching him with eyes that were blue at times and gray at times, and always gentle. More wood was put on the bivouac fire, and the flames grew ruddy. In their vivid light the young man did not seem quite so young. He had also a thick neck, great broad shoulders, and something of sensuality about the chin. The back of his skull was bulging and prominent. Here and there in his hair were little white streaks. Because there was such bloom and color in his cheeks, one could not remember these. Quantrell still tried to make out his face, to find a name for that Sphinx in front of him, to recall some time or circumstance, or place, that would make obscure things clear, and at last the past returned to him in the light of a swift revealment. "I have it all now," he said, "and you are a Jayhawker. The name is immaterial. I have seen you at Lawrence; I have seen you at Lane's headquarters; I have been a soldier myself with you; we have done duty together—but I have to hang you this hour, by G—d." Unabashed, the threatened man drew his breath hard and strode a step nearer Quantrell. Gregg put a pistol to his head. "Keep back. Can't you talk where you are? Do you mean to say anything?"

The old smile again; could anything ever drive away that smile—anything ever keep those teeth from shining? "You ask me if I want to talk, just as if I had anything to talk about. What can I say? I tell you that I have been hunted, proscribed, shot at, driven up and down, until I am tired. I want to kill somebody. I want to know what sleeping a sound night's sleep means." Quantrell's grave voice broke calmly in: "Bring a rope." Blunt brought it. "Make an end fast." The end was made fast to a low lying limb. In the firelight the noose expanded. "Up with him, men." Four stalwart hands seized him as a vice. He did not even defend himself. His flesh beneath their grip felt soft and rounded. The face, although all the bloom was there, hardened viciously—like the murderer's face it was. "So you mean to get rid of me that way? It is like you, Quantrell. I know you but you do not know me. I have been hunting you for three long years. You killed my brother in Kansas, you killed others there, your comrades. I did not know, till afterwards, what kind of a devil we had around our very messes—a devil who prowled about the camp fires and shot soldiers in the night that broke bread with him in the day. Can you guess what brought me here?"

The shifting phases of this uncommon episode attracted all; even Quantrell himself was interested. The prisoner—threw off all disguise and defied those who meant to hang him. "You did well to disarm me," he said, addressing Gregg, "for I intended to kill your captain. Everything has been against me. At the Tate house he escaped; at Clark's it was no better; we had him surrounded at Swearington's and his men cut him out; we ran him for two hundred miles and he escaped, and now after playing my last card and staking everything upon it, what is left to me?

A dog's death and a brother unavenged." "Do your worst," he said, and he folded his arms across his breast and stood stolid as the tree over his head. Some pity began to stir the men visibly. Gregg turned away and went out beyond the firelight. Even Quantrell's face softened, but only for a moment. Then he spoke harshly to Blunt, "He is one of the worst of a band that I failed to make a finish of before the war came, but what escapes today is dragged up by the next tomorrow. If I had not recognized him he would have killed me. I do not hang him for that, however, I hang him because the whole breed and race to which he belongs should be exterminated. Sergeant, do your duty." Blunt slipped the noose about the prisoner's neck, and the four men who had at first disarmed him, tightened it. To the last the bloom abode in his cheeks. He did not pray, neither did he make plaint nor moan. No man spoke a word. Something like a huge pendulum swung as though spun by a strong hand, quivered once or twice, and then swinging to and fro and regularly, stopped forever. Just at this moment three quick, hot vollies, and close together, rolled up from the northern picket post, and the camp was on its feet. If one had looked then at the dead man's face, something like a smile might have been seen there, fixed and sinister, and beneath it the white, sharp teeth. James Williams had accepted his fate like a hero. At mortal feud with Quantrell, and living only that he might meet him face to face in battle, he had joined every regiment, volunteered upon every scout, rode foremost in every raid, and fought hardest in every combat. It was not to be. Quantrell was leaving Missouri. A great gulf was about to separate them. One desperate effort now, and years of toil and peril at a single blow, might have been rewarded. He struck it and it cost him his life. To this day the whole tragic episode is sometimes recalled and discussed along the border.

The bivouac was rudely broken up. Three hundred Federal cavalry, crossing Quantrell's trail late in the afternoon, had followed it until the darkness fell, halted an hour for supper, and then again, at a good round trot, rode straight upon Haller, holding the rear of the movement southward. He fought at the outpost half an hour. Behind huge trees, he would not fall back until his flanks were in danger. All the rest of the night he fought them thus, making six splendid charges and holding on to every position until his grasp was broken loose by sheer hammering. At Grand River the pursuit ended and Quantrell swooped down upon Lamar, in Barton County, where a Federal garrison held the courthouse and the houses near it. He attacked but got worsted, and attacked again and lost one of his best men. He attacked the third time and made no better headway. He finally abandoned the town and resumed, unmolested, the road to the south. From Jackson County to the Arkansas line the whole country was swarming with militia and but for the fact that every Guerrilla was clad in Federal clothing, the march would have been an incessant battle. As it was, it will never be known how many isolated Federals, mistaking Quantrell's men for comrades of other regiments not on duty with them, fell into a trap that never gave up their victims alive. Near Cassville in Barry County, twenty-two were killed thus. They were coming up from Cassville and were meeting the Guerrillas, who were going south. The order given by Quantrell was a most simple one, but a most murderous one. By the side of each Federal in the approaching column a Guerrilla was to range himself, engage him in conversation, and then, at a given signal, blow his brains out. Quantrell gave the signal promptly, shooting the militiaman assigned to him through the middle of the forehead, and where, upon their horses, twenty-two confident men laughed and talked in comrade fashion a second before, nothing remained of the unconscious detachment, which was literally exterminated, save a few who straggled in agony upon the ground, and a mass of terrified and plunging horses. Not a Guerrilla missed his mark.

YOUNGER REMAINS IN MISSOURI WITH A SMALL DETACHMENT—WINTER OF 1862 AND 1863

THE remaining part of this chapter is the escapades of Cole Younger, who stayed in Missouri the winter of 1862 and 1863, with quite a number of the old band who were not in condition to ride when Quantrell and Captain Trow went south. But I know them to be true.

Younger was exceedingly enterprising, and fought almost daily. He did not seem to be affected by the severity of the winter, and at night, under a single blanket, he slept often in the snow while it was too bitter cold for Federal scouting parties to leave their comfortable cantonments or Federal garrisons to poke their noses beyond the snug surroundings of their well furnished barracks.

The Guerrilla rode everywhere and waylaid roads, bridges, lines of couriers and routes of travel. Six mail carriers disappeared in one week between Independence and Kansas City.

In a month after Quantrell arrived in Texas, George Todd returned to Jackson County, bringing with him Fletch Taylor, Boon Schull, James Little, Andy Walker and James Reed. Todd and Younger again came together by the bloodhound instinct which all men have who hunt or are hunted. Todd had scarcely made himself known to the Guerrilla in Jackson County before he had commenced to kill militiamen. A foraging party from Independence were gathering corn from a field belonging to Daniel White, a most worthy citizen of the vicinity, when Todd and Younger broke in upon it, shot five down in the field and put the rest to flight. Next day, November 30, 1862, Younger, having with him Josiah and Job McCockle and Tom Talley, met four of Jennison's regiment face to face in the neighborhood of the county poor house. Younger, who had an extraordinary voice, called out loud enough to be heard a mile, "You are four, and we are four. Stand until we come up." Instead of standing, however, the Jayhawkers turned about and rode off as rapidly as possible, followed by Younger and his men. All being excellently mounted, the ride lasted fully three miles before either party won or lost. At last the Guerrillas began to gain and kept gaining. Three of the four Jayhawkers were finally shot from their saddles and the fourth escaped by superior riding and superior running.

Todd, retaining with him those brought up from Arkansas, kept adding to them all who either from choice or necessity were forced to take refuge in the brush. Never happy except when on the war path, he suggested to Younger and

Cunningham a ride into Kansas City west of Little Santa Fe, always doubtful if not dangerous ground. Thirty Guerrillas met sixty-two Jayhawkers. It was a prairie fight, brief, bloody, and finished at a gallop. Todd's tactics, the old yell and the old rush, swept everything—a revolver in each hand, the bridle reins in his teeth, the horse at a full run, the individual rider firing right and left. This is the way the Guerrillas charged. The sixty-two Jayhawkers fought better than most of the militia had been in the habit of fighting, but they could not stand up to the work at revolver range. When Todd charged them furiously, which he did as soon as he came in sight of them, they stood a volley at one hundred yards and returned it, but not a closer grapple.

It was while holding the rear with six men that Cole Younger was attacked by fifty-two men and literally run over. In the midst of the *melee* bullets fell like hail stones in summer weather. John McDowell's horse went down, the rider under him and badly hit. He cried out to Younger for help. Younger, hurt himself and almost overwhelmed, dismounted under fire and rescued McDowell and brought him safely back from the furious crash, killing as he went a Federal soldier whose horse had carried him beyond Younger and McDowell who were struggling in the road together. Afterwards Younger was betrayed by the man to save whose life he had risked his own.

Divided again, and operating in different localities, Todd, Younger and Cunningham carried the terror of the Guerrilla name throughout the border counties of Kansas and Missouri. Every day, and sometimes twice a day, from December 3rd to December 18th, these three fought some scouting party or attacked some picket post. At the crossing of the Big Blue on the road to Kansas City—the place where the former bridge had been burned by Quantrell—Todd surprised six militiamen and killed them all and then hung them up on a long pole, resting it, either end upon forks, just as hogs are hung in the country after being slaughtered. The Federals, seeing this, began to get ready to drive them away from their lines of communication. Three heavy columns were sent out to scour the country. Surprising Cunningham in camp on Big Creek, they killed one of his splendid soldiers, Will Freeman, and drove the rest of the Guerrillas back into Jackson County.

Todd, joining himself quickly to Younger, ambuscaded the column hunting him, and in a series of combats between Little Blue and Kansas City, killed forty-seven of the pursuers, captured five wagons and thirty-three head of horses.

There was a lull again in marching and counter marching as the winter got colder and colder and some deep snow fell. Christmas time came, and the Guerrillas would have a Christmas frolic. Nothing bolder or braver is recorded upon the records of either side in the Civil War than this so-called Christmas frolic.

Colonel Henry Younger, father of Coleman Younger, was one of the most respected citizens of Western Missouri. He was a stalwart pioneer of Jackson County, having fourteen children born to him and his noble wife, a true Christian woman. A politician of the old school, Colonel Younger was for a number of years a judge of the county court of Jackson County, and for several terms was a member of the state legislature. In 1858, he left Jackson County for Cass County where he dealt largely in stock. He was also an extensive farmer, an enterprising merchant and the keeper of one of the best and most popular livery stables in the West, located at Harrisonville, the County seat of Cass County. His blooded horses were very superior, and he usually had on hand for speculative purposes amounts of money ranging from $6,000 to $10,000. On one of Jennison's periodical raides in the fall of 1862, he sacked and burned Harrisonville. Colonel Younger, although a staunch Union man, and known to be such, was made to lose heavily. Jennison and his officers took from him $4,000 worth of buggies, carriages and hacks and fifty head of blooded horses worth $500 each. Then the balance of his property that was perishable and not movable, was burned. The intention was to kill Colonel Younger, on the principle that dead men tell no tales, but he escaped with great difficulty and made his way to Independence. Jennison was told that Colonel Younger was rich and that he invariably carried with him large amounts of money. A plan was immediately laid to kill him. Twenty cut-throats were organized as a band, under a Jayhawker named Bailey, and set to watch his every movement. They dogged him from Independence to Kansas City and from Kansas City down to Cass County. Coming upon him at last in an isolated place within a few miles of Harrisonville, they riddled his body with bullets, rifled his pockets and left his body stark and partially stripped by the roadside.

Eight hundred Federals held Kansas City, and on every road was a strong picket post. The streets were patrolled continually, and ready always for an emergency. Horses saddled and bridled stood in their stalls.

Early on the morning of December 25th, 1862, Todd asked Younger if he would like to have a little fun. "What kind of fun?" the latter inquired. "A portion of the command that murdered your father are in Kansas City," said Todd, "and if you say so we will go into the place and kill a few of them." Younger caught eagerly at the proposition and commenced at once to get ready for the enterprise. Six were to compose the adventuresome party—Todd, Younger, Abe Cunningham, Fletch Taylor, Zach Traber and George Clayton. Clad in the uniform of the Federal cavalry, carrying instead of one pistol, four, they arrived about dusk at the picket post on the Westport and Kansas City road. They were not even halted. The uniform was a passport; to get in did not require a countersign. They left the horses in charge of Traber, bidding him do the best he could do if the worst came to the worst.

The city was filled with revelry. All the saloons were crowded. The five Guerrillas, with their heavy cavalry overcoats buttoned loosely about them, boldly walked down Main Street and into the Christmas revelry. Visiting this saloon and that saloon, they sat knee to knee with some of the Jennison men, some of Jennison's most blood-thirsty troopers, and drank confusion over and over again to the cut-throat Quantrell and his bushwhacking crew.

Todd knew several of the gang who had waylaid and slain Colonel Younger, but hunt how he could, he could not find a single man of them. Entering near onto midnight an ordinary drinking place near the public square, six soldiers were discovered sitting at two tables playing cards, two at one and four at another. A man and a boy were behind the bar. Todd, as he entered, spoke low to Younger.

TODD AND YOUNGER WENT TO KANSAS CITY TO HAVE A LITTLE FUN

"Run to cover at last. Five of the six men before you were in Bailey's crowd that murdered your father. How does your pulse feel?"

"Like an iron man's. I feel like I could kill the whole six myself."

They went up to the bar, called for whiskey and invited the card players to join. They did so.

If it was agreeable, the boy might bring their whiskey to them and the game could go on.

"Certainly," said Todd, with purring of a tiger cat ready for a spring, "that's what the boy is here for."

Over their whiskey the Guerrillas whispered. The killing now was as good as accomplished. Cunningham and Clayton were to saunter carelessly up to the table where the two players sat, and Todd, Younger and Taylor up to the table where the four sat. The signal to get ready was to be, "Come, boys, another drink," and the signal to fire was, "Who said drink?" Cole Younger was to give the first signal in his deep resonant voice and Todd the last one. After the first each Guerrilla was to draw a pistol and hold it under the cape of his cavalry coat and after the last he was to fire. Younger, as a special privilege, was accorded the right to shoot the sixth man. Cole Younger's deep voice broke suddenly in, filling all the room and sounding so jolly and clear. "Come, boys, another drink." Neither so loud nor so caressing as Younger's, yet sharp, distinct, and penetrating, prolonging, as it were, the previous proposition, and giving it emphasis, Todd exclaimed, "Who said drink?" A thunderclap, a single pistol shot, and then total darkness. The barkeeper dum in the presence of death, shivered and stood still. Todd, cool as a winter's night without, extinguished every light and stepped upon the street. "Steady," he said to his men, "do not make haste." So sudden had been the massacre, and so quick had been the movements of the Guerrillas, that the pursuers were groping for a clue and stumbling in their eagerness to find it. At every street corner an alarm was beating.

Past the press in the streets, past the glare and the glitter of the thicker lights, past patrol after patrol, Tod had won well his way to his horses when a black bar thrust itself suddenly across his path and changed itself instantly into a line of soldiers. Some paces forward a spokesman advanced and called a halt.

"What do you want?" asked Todd.

"The countersign."

"We have no countersign. Out for a lark, it's only a square or two further that we desire to go."

"No matter if its only an inch or two. Orders are orders."

"Fire; and charge men!" and the black line across the streets as a barricade shrivelled up and shrank away. Four did not move, however, nor would they ever move again, until, feet foremost, their comrades bore them to their burial place. But the hunt was hot. Mounted men were abroad, and hurrying feet could be heard in all directions. Rallying beyond range and reinforcements, the remnant of the patrol were advancing and opening fire. Born scout and educated Guerrilla, Traber—judging from the shots and shouts—knew what was best for all and dashed up to his hard-pressed comrades and horses. Thereafter the fight was a frolic. The picket on the Independence road was ridden over and through, and the brush beyond gained without an effort; and the hospitable house of Reuben Harris, where a roaring fire was blazing and a hearty welcome extended to all was reached.

In a week or less it began snowing. The hillsides were white with it. The nights were long, and the days bitter, and the snow did not melt. On the 10th of February, 1863, John McDowell reported his wife sick and asked Younger permission to visit her. The permission was granted, the proviso attached to it being the order to report again at 3 o'clock. The illness of the man's wife was a sham. Instead of going home, or even in the direction of home, he hastened immediately to Independence and made the commander there, Colonel Penick, thoroughly acquainted with Younger's camp and all its surroundings. Penick was a St. Joseph, Missouri, man, commanding a regiment of militia. The echoes of the desperate adventure of Younger and Todd in Kansas City had long ago reached the ears of Colonel Penick, and he seconded the traitor's story with an eagerness worthy the game to be hunted. Eighty cavalry, under a resolute officer, were ordered instantly out, and McDowell, suspected and closely guarded, was put at their head as a pilot.

Younger had two houses dug in the ground, with a ridge pole to each, and rafters. Upon the rafters were boards, and upon the boards straw and earth. At one end was a fireplace, at the other a door. Architecture was nothing, comfort everything.

The Federal officer dismounted his men two hundred yards from Younger's huts and divided them, sending forty to the south and forty to the north. The Federals on the north had approached to within twenty yards of Younger's cabins when a horse snorted fiercely and Younger came to the door of one of them. He saw the approaching column on foot and mistaking it for a friendly column, called out: "Is that you, Todd?" Perceiving his mistake, in a moment, however, he fired and killed the lieutenant in command of the attacking party and then aroused the men in the houses. Out of each the occupants poured, armed, desperate and determined to fight but never to surrender. Younger halted behind a tree and fought fifteen Federals for several moments, killed another who rushed upon him, rescued Hinton and strode away after his comrades, untouched and undaunted. Fifty yards further Tom Talley was in trouble. He had one boot off and one foot in the leg of the other, but try as he would he could get it neither off nor on. He could not run, situated as he was, and he had no knife to cut the leather. He too called out to Younger to wait for him and to stand by him until he could do something to extricate himself. Without hurry, and in the teeth of a rattling fusilade. Younger stooped to Talley's assistance, tearing literally from his foot by the exercise of immense strength the well-nigh fatal boot, and telling him to make the best haste he could and hold to his pistols. Braver man than Tom Talley never lived, nor cooler. As he jumped up in his stocking feet, the Federals were within twenty yards, firing as they advanced, and loading their breech loading guns as they ran. He took their fire at a range like that and snapped every barrel of his revolver in their faces. Not a cylinder exploded, being wet by the snow. He thus held in his hand a useless pistol. About thirty of the enemy had by this time outrun the rest and were forcing the fighting. Younger called to his men to take to the trees and drive them back, or stand and die together. The Guerrillas, hatless and some of them barefoot and coatless, rallied instantly and held their own. Younger killed two more of the pursuers here—five since the fighting began—and Bud Wigginton, like a lion at bay, fought without cover and with deadly effect. Here Job McCorkle was badly wounded, together with James Morris, John Coger and five others. George Talley, fighting splendidly, was shot dead, and Younger himself, encouraging his men by his voice and example, got a bullet through the left shoulder. The Federal advance fell back to the main body and the main body fell back to their horses.

A man by the name of Emmet Goss was now beginning to have it whispered of him that he was a tiger. He would fight, the Guerrillas said, and when in those savage days one went out upon the warpath so endorsed, be sure that it meant all that it was intended to mean. Goss lived in Jackson County. He owned a farm near Hickman's mill, and up to the fall of 1861, had worked it soberly and industriously. When he concluded to quit farming and go fighting, he joined the Jayhawkers. Jennison commanded the Fifteenth Kansas Cavalry, and Goss a company in this regiment. From a peaceful thrifty citizen he became suddenly a terror to the border. He seemed to have a mania for killing. Twenty odd unoffending citizens probably died at his hand. When Ewing's famous General Order No. 11 was issued—that order which required the wholesale depopulation of Cass, Bates, Vernon and Jackson Counties—Goss went about as a destroying angel, with a torch in one hand and a revolver in the other. He boasted of having kindled the fires in fifty-two houses, of having made fifty-two families homeless and shelterless, and of having killed, he declared, until he was tired of killing. Death was to come to him at last by the hand of Jesse James, but not yet.

Goss had sworn to capture or kill Cole Younger, and went to the house of Younger's mother on Big Creek for the purpose. She was living in a double log cabin built for a tenant, by her husband before his death, and Cole was at home. It was about eight o'clock and quite dark. Cole sat talking with his mother, two little sisters and a boy brother. Goss, with forty men, dismounted back from the yard, fastened their horses securely, moved up quietly and surrounded the house.

Between the two rooms of the cabin there was an open passageway, and the Jayhawkers had occupied this before the alarm was given. Desiring to go from one room to another, a Miss Younger found the porch full of armed men. Instantly springing back and closing the door, she shouted Cole's name, involuntarily. An old negro woman—a former slave—with extraordinary presence of mind, blew out the light, snatched a coverlet from the bed, threw it over her head and shoulders.

"Get behind me, Marse Cole, quick," she said in a whisper.

And Cole, in a second, with a pistol in each hand, stood close up to the old woman, the bed spread covering them both. Then throwing wide the door, and receiving in her face the gaping muzzles of a dozen guns, she querously cried out:

"Don't shoot a poor old nigger, Massa Sogers. Its nobody but me going to see what's de matter. Ole missus is nearly scared to death."

Slowly, then, so slowly that it seemed an age to Cole, she strode through the crowd of Jayhawkers blocking up the portico, and out into the darkness and night. Swarming about the two rooms and rumaging everywhere, a portion of the Jayhawkers kept looking for Younger, and swearing brutally at their ill-success, while another portion, watching the movements of the old negress, saw her throw away the bed-spread, clap her hands exultantly and shout: "Run, Marse Cole; run for your life. The debbils can't catch you dis time!"

Giving and taking a volley that harmed no one, Cole made his escape without a struggle. As for the old negress, Goss debated sometime with himself whether he should shoot her or hang her. Unquestionably a rebel negro, she was persecuted often and often for her opinion's sake, and hung up twice by militia to make her tell the whereabouts of Guerrillas. True to her people and her cause, she died at last in the ardor of devotion.

THE TRIP NORTH IN 1863

ON the return from Texas in the spring of 1863, Quantrell's journey in detail would read like a romance. The whole band, numbering thirty, were clad in Federal uniforms, Quantrell wearing that of a captain. Whenever questioned, the answer was, "A Federal scout on special service." Such had been the severity of the winter, and such the almost dead calm in military quarters, that all ordinary vigilance seemed to have relaxed and even ordinary prudence forgotten.

South of Spring River a day's march, ten militia came upon Quantrell's camp and invited themselves to supper. They were fed, but they were also killed. Quantrell himself was the host. He poured out the coffee, supplied attentively every little want, insisted that those whose appetites were first appeased should eat more, and then shot at his table the two nearest to him and saw the others fall beneath the revolvers of his men, with scarcely so much as a change of color in his face.

North of Spring River there was a dramatic episode. Perhaps in those days every country had its tyrants. Most generally revolutions breed monsters.

On the way to Missouri, they fell in with Marmaduke, who was commanding a bunch of Bushwhackers in St. Claire County, Missouri. He also had been wintering in Texas, and they camped one night near us. Marmaduke was telling Quantrell about an old Federal captain named Obediah Smith—what a devil he was and how he was treating the Southern people. Quantrell laughed and asked:

"Why don't you kill him?"

Marmaduke said he was too sharp and cunning for him.

Quantrell said, "If you will detail one or two of your men to come with me and show me where he lives, I will kill him with his own gun."

It being agreed upon, the next morning Marmaduke called on Oliver Burch to pilot Quantrell to where Smith lived. The following morning all marched up to within about a mile or so of where Captain Smith lived. Quantrell called his men together, chose Wash Haller, Dick Burns, Ben Morrow, Dick Kenney, Frank James and myself of his own command, and Oliver Burch of Marmaduke's command. They rode up to Captain Smith's house, all dressed in Federal uniforms, and called at the gate, "Hello." Smith came walking out and Quantrell saluted him and told him he was a scout for the Federals from Colonel Penick's army. Smith saw them in the same uniform as himself and did not once think of their betraying him. They talked for a few minutes when Quantrell said:

"Captain, that is a fine gun you have there; why don't you furnish us scouts with a gun like that."

"This is a fine gun," replied Smith, "it has killed lots of d— —d bushwhackers."

Quantrell said, "Captain, would you mind letting me see that gun?"

Taking it from him, Quantrell began to look it over, and turning to his pals, said, "Ain't that a dandy?"

They all answered, "Yes, wish I had one."

Quantrell kept fooling with the gun and, catching Captain Smith's eye off him, fired it at him, shooting him through the heart and killing him instantly. Killing Smith was getting rid of one of the worst men in Cedar County.

That day about ten o'clock, three militiamen came to the column and were killed. A mile from where dinner was procured, five more came out. These also were killed. In the dusk of the evening two more were killed, and where we bivouacked, one was killed. The day's work counted eleven in the aggregate, and nothing of an exertion to find a single soldier made, at that.

Evil tidings were abroad, however—evil things that took wings and flew as birds. Some said from the first that Quantrell's men were not Union men and some swore that no matter what kind of clothing they wore, those inside of said clothing were wolves. Shot evenly; that is to say, by experienced hands, in the head, the corpses of the first discovered ten awakened from their sleep the garrison along the Spring River. Smith's execution stirred them to aggression, and the group of dead militiamen crossed continually upon the roadside, while it enraged it also horrified every cantonment or camp. Two hundred cavalrymen got quickly to horse and poured up from the rear after Quantrell. It was not difficult to keep on his track. Here a corpse and there a corpse, here a heap and there a heap—blue always, and blue continually—what manner of a wild beast had been sent out from the unknown to prey upon the militia?

At the Osage River the Federal pursuit, gathering volume and intensity as it advanced, struck Quantrell hard and brought him to an engagement south of the river. Too much haste, however, cost him dearly. The advance, being the smaller, had outridden the main army and was unsupported and isolated when attacked. Quantrell turned upon it savagely and crushed it at a blow. Out of sixty-six troopers he killed twenty. In those days there were no wounded. Before the main body came up he was over the Osage and away, and riding fast to encompass the immense prairie between the river and Johnstown. When scarcely over it, a flanking column made a dash at him coming from the west, killed Blunt's horse and drove Quantrell to timber. Night fell and he rode out of sight and out of hearing. When he drew rein again it was at the farm of Judge Russell Hicks on the Sni, in Jackson County. The next morning at David George's he disbanded for ten days, sending messengers out in all directions to announce his arrival and make known the rendezvous.

The ten days allotted by Quantrell for concentration purposes had not yet expired, but many of the reckless spirits, rapacious for air and exercise, could not be kept still. Poole, Ross and Greenwood made a dash for the German settlement of

Lafayette County, and left some marks there that are not yet obliterated. Albert Cunningham, glorying in the prowess of a splendid manhood, and victor in a dozen combats against desperate odds, fell before the spring came, in an insignificant skirmish on the Harrisonville and Pleasant Hill road.

In the lull of military movements in Jackson County, Cass was to see the inauguration of the heavy Guerrilla work of 1863. Three miles west of Pleasant Springs, Younger and his comrades struck a blow that had the vigor of the olden days in it. The garrison at Pleasant Hill numbered three hundred, and from the garrison of Lieutenant Jefferson took thirty-two cavalrymen and advanced three miles towards Smith's, on a scouting expedition. While Hulse and Noah Webster, two Guerrilas who seemed never to sleep and to be continually hanging about the flanks of the Federals, discovered Jefferson and reported his movements to the main body encamped at Parson Webster's. Taking with him eight men, Joe Lee hurried to cut Jefferson off from Pleasant Hill. Younger, with eight more, was close up from the west. Lee had with him John Webster, Noah Webster, Sterling Kennedy, David Kennedy, William Hays, Perry Hays, Henry McAninch, James Marshall, Edward Marshall and Edward Hink. He was to gain the east end of the lane and halt there until Younger came up at its western extremity. Jefferson discovered Lee, however, and formed a line of battle in front of Smith's, throwing some skirmishers forward and getting ready apparently for a fight, although afterwards it was reported that Lee's men were mistaken for a portion of the garrison left behind at Pleasant Hill. Younger had further to go than he at first supposed, but was making all the haste possible, when Lee, carried away by the uncontrolable impulse of his men, charged down the lane from the east, at a furious rate. Jefferson held his troopers fair to their line, until the Guerrillas reached a carbine range, but could hold them no longer. A volley and a stampede and the wild race was on again. About a length ahead and splendidly mounted, William Hays led the Guerrillas. Shot dead, his horse fell from under him and crushed his senses out for half an hour. John and Noah Webster took Hays' place through sheer superiority of horse flesh and forced the fighting, John killing three of the enemy as he ran and Noah, four. Noah's pistols were empty, but he dashed alongside of the rearmost trooper and knocked him from his saddle with the butt of one of them, and seized another by the collar of his coat and dragged him to the ground. Both were dispatched. Too late to block the western mouth of the lane, Younger joined in the swift pursuit as it passed him to the left and added much to the certainty of the killing. Of the thirty-two, four alone escaped, and Jefferson was not among them. Hulse shot him running at a distance of fifty yards, and before he got to him he was dead.

Pleasant Hill was instantly evacuated. Not a Federal garrison remained in Cass, outside of Harrisonville, and the garrison there was as effectively imprisoned as if surrounded by the walls of a fortress. The Guerrillas rode at ease in every direction.

Younger and Lon Railey hung about the town for a week killing its pickets and destroying its foraging parties. Other bands in other directions gathered up valuable horses for future service and helped onward to the southern army troops of recruits who needed only pilots and protection to the Osage River.

Like Cunningham, the man who had fought as a lion in twenty different combats, was destined to fall in a sudden and unnoted skirmish. Returning northward in the rear of Quantrell, Lieutenant William Haller was attacked at sunset and fought till dark. He triumphed, but he fell. His comrades buried him and wept for him, and left him.

The battle of the year 1863 had commenced; formidable men were coming to the surface in every direction. Here and there sudden Guerrilla fires leaped up from many places about the State, and burned as if fed by oil, until everything in their reach had been consumed. It was a year of savage fighting and killing; it was the year of the torch and the black flag; it was the year when the invisible reaper reaped sorest in the ranks of the Guerrillas and gathered into harvest sheaves, the bravest of the brave.

Anderson, newly coming into sight, was flashing across the military horizon as a war comet. Left to himself and permitted to pursue his placid ways in peace, probably the amiable neighbor and working man would never have been developed into a tiger. But see how he was wrought upon! One day late in 1862, a body of Federal soldiers, especially enrolled and uninformed to persecute women and prey upon non-combatants, gathered up in a half day's raid a number of demonstrative Southern girls whose only sin had been extravagant talk and pro-Confederacy cheering. They were taken to Kansas City and imprisoned in a dilapidated tenement close upon a steep place. Food was flung to them at intervals, and brutal guards sang ribald songs and used indecent language in their presence. With these women, tenderly nurtured and reared, were two of Will Anderson's sisters. Working industriously in Kansas with his father, Anderson knew nothing of the real struggles of the war, nor of the imprisonment of his sisters. A quiet, courteous, fair-minded man who took more delight in a book than in a crowd, he had a most excellent name in Randolph County, Missouri, where he was born, and in Johnson County, Kansas, where he was living in 1862. Destiny had to deal with him, however. The old rickety, ramshackle building in which were the huddled women, did not fall down fast enough for the brutes who bellowed about it. At night and in the darkness it was undermined, and in the morning when a little wind blew upon it and it was shaken, it fell with a crash. Covered up, the faces disfigured, the limp, lifeless bodies were past all pain! Dead to touch, or kiss, or passionate entreaty, Anderson's eldest sister was taken from the ruins a corpse. The younger, badly injured in the spine, with one leg broken and her face bruised and cut painfully, lived to tell the terrible story of it all to a gentle, patient brother kneeling before her at her bedside and looking up above to see if God were there.

Soon a stir came along the border. A name new to the strife was beginning to pass from band to band and about the camp fires to have a respectful hearing.

"Anderson?" "Anderson?" "Who is this Anderson?" The Guerrillas asked one of another. "He kills them all. Quantrell spares now and then, and Poole and Blunt, and Yager, and Haller, and Jarrette, and Younger, and Gregg, and Todd, and Shepherd, and all the balance; but Anderson, never. Is he a devil in uniform?"

JESSE JAMES JOINS COMMAND

JESSE JAMES, younger brother of Frank James, had now emerged from the awkwardness of youth. He was scarcely thirteen years of age, while Frank was four years older. The war made them Guerrillas. Jesse was at home with his stepfather, Dr. Reuben Samuels, of Clay County. He knew nothing of the strife save the echoes of it now and then as it reached his mother's isolated farm. One day a company of militia visited this farm, hanged Dr. Samuels to a tree until he was left for dead, and seized upon Jesse, a mere boy in the fields plowing, put a rope about his neck and abused him harshly, pricking him with sabers, and finally threatening him with death should they ever again hear of his giving aid or information to the Guerrillas. That same week his mother and sisters were arrested, carried to St. Joseph and thrown into a filthy prison, where the hardships they endured were dreadful. Often without adequate food, insulted by sentinels who neither understood nor cared to learn the first lesson of a soldier—courtesy to women—cut off from all communication with the world, the sister was brought near to death's door from a fever which followed the punishment, while the mother—a high spirited and courageous matron—was released only after suffering and emaciation had aged her in her prime. Before Mrs. Samuels returned to her home, Jesse had joined Frank in the camp of Quantrell, who had preceded him a few years, and who had already, notwithstanding the briefness of his service, made a name for supreme and conspicuous daring. Jesse James had a face as smooth and innocent as the face of a school girl. The blue eyes, very clear and penetrating, were never at rest. His form, tall and finely moulded—was capable of great effort and great endurance. On his lips there was always a smile, and for every comrade a pleasant word or a compliment. Looking at the small white hands with their long, tapering fingers, it was not then written or recorded that they were to become with a revolver among the quickest and deadliest hands in the West. Frank was four years older, and somewhat taller than Jesse. Jesse's face was something of an oval; Frank's was long, wide about the forehead, square and massive about the jaw and chin, and set always in a look of fixed repose. Jesse laughed at many things; Frank laughed not at all. Jesse was light hearted, reckless, devil-may-care; Frank sober, sedate, a splendid man always for ambush or scouting parties.

Scott had to come back from the South and, eager for action, crossed the Missouri River at Sibley May 20, 1863, taking with him twelve men. Frank James and James Little led the advance. Beyond the river thirteen miles, and at the house of Moses McCoy, the Guerrillas camped, concocting a plan whereby the Federal garrison at Richfield, numbering thirty, might be got at and worsted.

Captain Sessions was in command at Richfield, and his grave had already been dug. Scott found a friendly citizen named Peter Mahoney who volunteered to do the decoy work. He loaded up a wagon with wood, clothed himself in the roughest and raggedest clothes he had, and rumbled away behind as scrawny and fidgety a yoke of oxen as ever felt a north wind in the winter bite their bones, or deceptive buckeye in the spring swell their body.

"Mr. Mahoney, what is the news?" This was the greeting he got.

"No news, I have wood for sale. Yes, there is some news, too. I like to have forgot. Eight or ten of those Quantrell men are prowling about my way, the infernal scoundrels, and I hope they may be hunted out of the country."

Mahoney did well, but Scott did better. He secreted his men three miles from Richfield, and near the crossing of a bridge. If an enemy came the bridge was a sentinel—its resounding planks, the explosion of a musket. Scott, with eight men, dismounted and lay close along the road. Gregg, with Fletch Taylor, James Little and Joe Hart, mounted and ready to charge, kept still and expectant fifty yards in the rear in ambush. Presently at the crossing a dull booming was heard, and the Guerrillas knew that Sessions had bit at the bait Mahoney offered. A sudden clinking along the line—the eight were in a hurry.

"Be still," said Scott; "You cock too soon. I had rather have two cool men than ten impatient ones."

The Federals came right onward; they rode along gaily in front of the ambuscade; they had no skirmishers out and they were doomed. The leading files were abreast of Scott on the right when he ordered a volley, and Sessions, Lieutenant Graffenstein and seven privates fell dead. What was left of the Federal array turned itself into a rout; Gregg, Taylor, Little, and Hart thundered down to the charge. Scott mounted again, and altogether and away at a rush, pursuers and pursued dashed into Richfield. The remnant of the wreck surrendered, and Scott, more merciful than many among whom he soldiered, spared the prisoners and paroled them.

HOUSE OCCUPIED BY WOMEN LIGHT OF LOVE

Four miles from Independence, and a little back from the road leading to Kansas City, stood a house occupied by several women light of love. Thither regularly went Federal soldiers from the Independence garrison, and the drinking was deep and the orgies shameful. Gregg set a trap to catch a few of the comers and goers. Within the lines of the enemy much circumspection was required to make an envelopment of the house successful. Jesse James was chosen from among the number of volunteers and sent forward to reconnoiter the premises. Jesse, arrayed in coquettish female apparel, with his smooth face, blue eyes, and blooming cheeks, looked the image of a bashful country girl, not yet acquainted with vice, though half eager and half reluctant to walk a step nearer to the edge of its perilous precipice. As he mounted, woman fashion, upon a fiery horse, the wind blew all about his peach colored face the pink ribbons of a garish bonnet and lifted the tell-tale riding habit just enough to reveal instead of laced shoes or gaiters, the muddy boots of a born cavalryman. Gregg, taking twelve men, followed in the rear of

James to within a half a mile of the nearest picket post and hid in the woods until word could be brought from the bagnio ahead. If by a certain hour the disguised Guerilla did not return to his comrades, the pickets were to be driven in, the house surrounded, and the inmates forced to give such information as they possessed, of his whereabouts.

Jesse James, having pointed out to him with tolerable accuracy the direction of the house, left the road, skirted the timber rapidly, leaped several ravines, floundered over a few marshy places and finally reached his destination without meeting a citizen or encountering an enemy. He would not dismount, but sat upon his horse at the fence and asked that the mistress of the establishment might come out to him. Little by little, and with many gawky protests and many a bashful simper, he told a plausible story of parental *espionage* and family discipline. He, ostensibly a she, could not have a beau, could not go with the soldiers, could not sit with them late, nor ride with them, nor romp with them. She was tired of it all and wanted a little fun. Would the mistress let her come to her house occasionally and bring some of the neighborhood girls with her, who were in the same predicament? The mistress laughed and was glad. New faces to her were like new coin, and she put forth a hand and patted the merchantable thing upon the knee, and ogled her smiling mouth and girlish features gleefully. As the she-wolf and venturesome lamb separated, the assignation was assured. That night the amorous country girl, accompanied by three of her female companions, was to return, and the mistress, confident of her ability to provide lovers was to make known among the soldiers the attractive acquisition.

It lacked an hour of sunset when Jesse James got back to Gregg; an hour after sunset the Guerrillas, following hard upon the tracks made by the boy spy, rode rapidly on to keep the trysting place. The house was aglow with lights and jubilant with laughter. Drink abounded, and under cover of the clinking glasses, the men kissed the women. Anticipating the orgy of unusual attraction, twelve Federals had been lured out from the garrison and made to believe that barefoot maidens ran wild in the woods and buxom lasses hid for the hunting. No guards were out; no sentinels posted. Jesse James crept close to a window and peered in. The night was chilly and a large wood fire blazed upon a large hearth. All the company were in one room, five women and a dozen men. Scattered about, yet ready for the grasping, the cavalry carbines were in easy reach, and the revolvers handy about the persons. Sampson trusting everything to Delilah, might not have trusted so much if under the old dispensation there had been anything of bushwhacking.

Gregg loved everybody who wore the gray, and what exercised him most was the question just now of attack. Should he demand a surrender? Jesse James, the boy, said no to the veteran. Twelve men inside the house, and the house inside their own lines where reinforcements might be hurried quickly to them, would surely hold their own against eleven outside, if indeed they did not make it worse. The best thing to do was to fire through the windows and kill what could be killed by a carbine volley, then rush through the door and finish, under the cover of the smoke, horror and panic, those who should survive the broadside.

JESSE JAMES GOING TO HOUSE OF LIGHT OF LOVE

Luckily the women sat in a corner to themselves and close to a large bed fixed to the wall and to the right of the fireplace. On the side of the house the bed was on, two broad windows opened low upon the ground, and between the windows there was a door, not ajar, but not fastened. Gregg, with five men, went to the upper window, and Taylor, with four, took possession of the lower. The women were out of immediate range. The house shook; the glass shivered, the door was hurled backward, there was a hot stifling crash of revolvers; and on the dresses of the women and the white coverlet of the bed great red splotches. Eight out of the twelve fell dead or wounded at the first fire; after the last fire all were dead. It was a spectacle ghastly beyond any ever witnessed by the Guerrillas, because so circumscribed. Piled two deep the dead men lay, one with a glass grasped tightly in his stiffened fingers, and one in his shut hand the picture of a woman scantily clad. How they wept, the poor, painted things, for the slain soldiers, and how they blasphemed; but Gregg tarried not, neither did he make atonement. As they lay there heaped where they fell and piled together, so they lay still when he mounted and rode away.

In the three months preceding the Lawrence massacre, over two hundred citizens were killed and their property burned or stolen. In mid-winter houses were burned by the hundred and whole neighborhoods devastated and laid waste. Aroused as he had never been before, Quantrell meditated a terrible vengeance.

LAWRENCE MASSACRE

IN the spring of 1863, Quantrell issued a proclamation to the Federal forces of Kansas that if they did not stop burning and robbing houses, killing old men and women, he would in return come to Lawrence at some unexpected time and paint the city blacker than hades and make its streets run with blood.

On Blackwater, in Johnson County, and at the house of Captain Purdee, Quantrell called the Guerrillas together for the Lawrence massacre. Todd, Jarrette, Blunt, Gregg, Trow, Anderson, Yager, Younger, Estes and Holt, all were there, and when the roll was called three hundred and ten answered promptly to their names. Up to the mustering hour Quantrell had probably not let his left hand know what his right hand had intended. Secrecy necessarily was to be the salvation of the expedition, if indeed there was any salvation for it. The rendezvous night was an August night—a blessed, balmy, mid-summer night—just such a night as would be chosen to give force to reflections and permit the secrets of the soul to escape. The sultry summer day had lain swarthily in the sun and panting; the sultry summer winds had whispered nothing of the shadowy woods, nothing of the babble of unseen brooks. Birds spoke goodbye to birds in the tree tops, and the foliage was filled with twilight. Quantrell sat grave and calm in the midst of his chieftains who were grouped about him. Further away where the shadows were, the men massed themselves in silent companies or spoke low to one another, and briefly. Something of a foreboding, occult though it was, and undefinable, made itself manifest. The shadow of a great tragedy was impending.

Without in the least degree minimizing or magnifying the difficulties of the undertaking, Quantrell laid before his officers his plans for attacking Lawrence. For a week a man of the command—a cool, bold, plausible, desperate man—had been in the city—thought it, over it, about it and around it—and he was here in their midst to speak. Would they listen to him?

"Let him speak," said Todd, sententiously.

Lieutenant Fletcher Taylor came out from the shadow, bowed gravely to the group, and with the brevity of a soldier who knew better how to fight than to talk, laid bare the situation. Disguised as a stock trader, or rather, assuming the role of a speculating man, he had boldly entered Lawrence. Liberal, for he was bountifully supplied with money; keeping open rooms at the Eldridge House, and agreeable in every way and upon every occasion, he had seen all that it was necessary to see, and learned all that could be of any possible advantage to the Guerrillas. The city proper was but weakly garrisoned; the camp beyond the river was not strong; the idea of a raid by Quantrell was honestly derided; the streets were broad and good for charging horsemen, and the hour for the venture was near at hand.

"You have heard the report," Quantrell said with a deep voice, "but before you decide it is proper that you should know it all. The march to Lawrence is a long one; in every little town there are soldiers; we leave soldiers behind us; we march through soldiers; we attack the town garrisoned by soldiers; we retreat through soldiers; and when we would rest and refit after the exhaustive expedition, we have to do the best we can in the midst of a multitude of soldiers. Come, speak out, somebody. What is it, Anderson?"

"Lawrence or hell, but with one proviso, that we kill every male thing."

"Todd?"

"Lawrence, if I knew not a man would get back alive."

"Gregg?"

"Lawrence, it is the home of Jim Lane; the foster mother of the Red Legs; the nurse of the Jayhawkers."

"Shepherd?"

"Lawrence. I know it of old; 'niggers' and white men are just the same there; its a Boston colony and it should be wiped out."

"Jarrette?"

"Lawrence, by all means. I've had my eye on it for a long time. The head devil of all this killing and burning in Jackson County; I vote to fight it with fire—to burn it before we leave it."

"Dick Maddox?"

"Lawrence; and an eye for an eye and a tooth for a tooth; God understands better than we do the equilibrium of Civil War."

"Holt?"

"Lawrence, and be quick about it."

"Yager?"

"Where my house once stood there is a heap of ruins. I haven't a neighbor that's got a house—Lawrence and the torch."

"Blunt?"

"Count me whenever there is killing. Lawrence first and then some other Kansas town; the name is nothing."

"Have you all voted?"

"All."

"Then Lawrence it is; saddle up, men!"

Thus was the Lawrence Massacre inaugurated.

Was it justifiable? Is there much of anything that is justifiable in Civil War? Originally, the Jayhawkers in Kansas had been very poor. They coveted the goods of their Missouri neighbors, made wealthy or well-to-do by prosperous years of peace and African slavery. Before they became soldiers they had been brigands, and before they destroyed houses in the name of retaliation they had plundered them at the instance of personal greed. The first Federal officers operating in Kansas; that is to say, those who belonged to the state, were land pirates or pilferers. Lane was a wholesale plunderer; Jennison, in the scaly gradation, stood next to Lane; Anthony next to Jennison; Montgomery next to Anthony; Ransom next to Montgomery, and so on down until it reached to the turn of captains, lieutenants, sergeants, corporals and privates. Stock in herds, droves and multitudes were driven from Missouri into Kansas. Houses gave up their furniture; women, their jewels; children, their wearing apparel; store-rooms, their contents; the land, their crops, and the banks, their deposits. To robbery was added murder; to murder, arson, and to arson depopulation. Is it any wonder, then, that the Missourian whose father was killed should kill in return, whose house was burnt should burn in return, whose property was plundered, should pillage in return, whose life was made miserable, should hunt as a wild beast and rend accordingly? Many such were in Quantrell's command—many whose lives were blighted; who in a night were made orphans and paupers; who saw the labor and accumulation of years swept away in an hour of wanton destruction; who for no reason on earth save that they were Missourians, were hunted from hiding place to hiding place; who were preyed upon while not a single cow remained or a single shock of grain; who were shot at, bedeviled and proscribed, and who, no matter whether Union or disunion, were permitted to have neither flag nor country.

It was the summer night of August 16, 1863, that the Guerilla column, having at its head its ominous banner, marched west from Purdee's place on Blackwater. With its simple soldiers, or rather volunteers for the expedition, were Colonels Joseph Holt and Boaz Roberts. Officers of the regular Confederate army, who were in Missouri on recruiting service when the march began, fell into line as much from habit as from inclination.

The first camp was made upon a stream midway between Pleasant Hill and Lone Jack, where the grazing was good and the hiding places excellent. All day Quantrell concealed himself there, getting to saddle just at dark and ordering Todd up from the rear to the advance. Passing Pleasant Hill to the north and marching on rapidly fifteen miles, the second camp was at Harrelson's, twenty-five miles from the place of starting. At three o'clock in the afternoon of the second day, the route was resumed and followed due west to Aubrey, a pleasant Kansas stream, abounding in grass and timber. Here Quantrell halted until darkness set in, feeding the horses well and permitting the men to cook and eat heartily. At eight o'clock the march began again and continued on throughout the night, in the direction of Lawrence. Three pilots were pressed into service, carried with the command as far as they knew anything of the road or the country, and then shot down remorselessly in the nearest timber.

On the morning of the 21st, Lawrence was in sight. An old man a short distance upon the right of the road was feeding his hogs in the gray dawn, the first person seen to stir about the doomed place. Quantrell sent Cole Younger over to the hog-pen to catechize the industrious old farmer and learn from him what changes had taken place in the situation since Taylor had so thoroughly accomplished his mission. Younger, dressed as a Federal lieutenant, exhausted speedily the old man's limited stock. Really, but little change had taken place. Across the Kansas river there were probably four hundred soldiers in camp, and on the Lawrence side about seventy-five. As for the rebels, he didn't suppose there was one nearer than Missouri; certainly none within striking distance of Lawrence.

It was a lovely morning. The green of the fields and the blue of the skies were glad together. Birds sang sweetly. The footsteps of autumn had not yet been heard in the land.

"The camp first," was the cry which ran through the ranks, and Todd, leading Quantrell's old company, dashed down, yelling and shooting. Scarcely any resistance was made, as every time they stuck their heads out of a tent it was met with a bullet. Ridden over, shot in their blankets, paralyzed, some of them with terror, they ran frantically about. What could they do against the quickest and deadliest pistol shots along the border?

Bill Anderson, Todd, Jarrette, Little, McGuire, Long, Bill McGuire, Richard Kenney, Allen Parmer, Frank James, Clemmons, Shepherd, Hinton, Blunt, Harrison Trow, and the balance of the older men did the most of the killing. They went for revenge, and they took it. These men killed. They burned. The Federals on the opposite side of the river made scarcely any attempt to come to the rescue of their butchered comrades. A few skirmishes held them in check. It was a day of darkness and woe. Killing ran riot. The torch was applied to every residence; the air was filled with cries for mercy; dead men lay in cellars, upon streets, in parlors where costly furniture was, on velvet carpets. The sun came up and flooded the sky with its radiance and yet the devil's work was not done. Smoke ascended into the air, and the crackling of blazing rafters and crashing of falling walls filled the air. A true story of the day's terrible work will never be told. Nobody knows it. It is a story of episodes, tragic—a story full of collossal horrors and unexpected deliverances.

Frank James, just as he was in the act of shooting a soldier in uniform who had been caught in a cellar—his pistol was at the Federal's head—heard an exceedingly soft and penetrating voice calling out to him, "Do not kill him for my sake. He has eight children who have no mother." James looked and saw a beautiful girl just turned sixteen, blushing at her boldness and trembling before him. In the presence of so much grace and loveliness her father was disarmed. He remembered his own happy youth, his sister, not older than the girl beside him, his mother who had always instilled into his mind lessons of mercy and charity. He put up his pistol.

"Take him, he is yours. I would not harm a hair of his head for the whole state of Kansas," said James.

Judge Carpenter was killed in the yard of H. C. Clark, and Colonel Holt, one of the Confederate officers with the expedition, saved Clark. He saved others besides Clark. He had been a Union man doing business in Vernon County, Missouri, as a merchant. Jennison, belonging to old Jim Lane of Lawrence, noted "nigger" thief, robber and house burner, who always ran from the enemy, raided the neighborhood in which he lived, plundered him of his goods, burnt his property, insulted his family, and Holt joined the Confederate army for revenge. The notorious general, James H. Lane, to get whom Quantrell would gladly have left and sacrificed the balance of the victims, made his escape through a corn field, hotly pursued but too speedily mounted to be captured. He swam the river.

There were two camps in Lawrence at the time of the attack, one camp of the "nigger" troops being located at the southern end of Massachusetts street and the other camp of white soldiers were camped in the heart of the city. In this latter camp there were twenty-one infantry, eighteen of whom were killed in the first wild charge.

Cole Younger had dragged from his hiding place in a closet a very large man who had the asthma. In his fright and what with his hurry the poor man could not articulate. Younger's pistol was against his heart when his old wife cried out, "For God's sake, do not shoot him. He has not slept in a bed for nine years." This appeal and the asthma together, caused Younger to roar out, "I never intended to harm a hair of his head."

Todd and Jarrette, while roaming through Eldridge's house in search of adventure, came upon a door that was locked. Todd knocked and cried out that the building was in flames and it was time to get away. "Let it burn and be d— —d," a deep voice answered, and then the voices of three men were heard in conversation. Jarrette threw his whole weight against the door, bursting it open, and as he did so Todd fired and killed one of the three, Jarrette another and Todd the third, who were hiding there. They were soldiers who had escaped in the morning's massacre, and who did not even make an effort to defend themselves. Perhaps the number killed will never be accurately known, but I should say there were at least one thousand killed, and none wounded. The loss of property amounted to the enormous sum of $1,500,000. The total buildings consumed were one hundred and eighty-nine. In the city proper Quantrell had one man killed and two wounded. The man who lost his life was drunk when the firing began. His name was Larkin Skaggs, and the fighting at Lawrence was the first he had ever done as a Guerilla.

Fate favored Quantrell from the time he left Missouri until he returned to Missouri. A man from Johnson County, Kansas, started by an Indian trail to inform the people of Lawrence of his coming. He rode too carelessly and his horse fell and so injured him that he died. A full company of soldiers were situated at Oxford, but they seemed more anxious to keep out of the way than to fight.

As Quantrell retreated from Lawrence, he sat upon the right end, William Gregg with twenty men upon the left. Bill Anderson with twenty men, Gregg took with him Frank James, Arch Clemmons, Little, Morrow, Harrison Trow and others of the most desperate men of the band. Anderson took Hockinsmith, Long, McGuire, Parmer, Hicks, Hi George, Doc Campbell and other equally desperate characters. Each was ordered to burn a swath as they marched back parallel with the main body and to kill in proportion as he burned. Soon on every hand were columns of smoke beginning to rise, and soon was heard the rattle of firing arms from around the consuming houses, and old farmers who had taken up arms were shot down as a holiday frolic. This unforgiving farewell lasted for twelve miles until pressed too heavily in the rear. Quantrell was forced to recall his detachments and look to the safety of his aggregate columns.

Missouriward from Kansas ten miles, Quantrell halted to rest and eat a little. Cole Younger rode out into a cabbage patch and got himself a cabbage head and began to eat it. The lady of the house came out. Younger said:

"This is a very fine cabbage you have." The lady replied:

"I hope it will choke you to death, you d——d old rebel son-of-a-buck."

"Thank you, ma'am," was the reply. "Where is your husband?"

Before any of the men had finished eating, the pickets were drawn into the rear, pressed to the girth. Todd and Jarrette held out as two lines that had not broken fast. Step by step, and firing at everyone in pursuit, at arm's length, for ten miles further the Federals would not charge. Overwhelming in numbers though they were, and capable of taking at any moment everything in opposition to them, they contented themselves with firing at long range and keeping always at and about a deadly distance from the rear. The Guerillas, relying principally upon dash and revolver, felt the need of a charge. Quantrell halted the whole column for a charge. The detachments on either flank had some time since been gathered up and the men brought face to face with urgent need. Turned about quickly and dressed up in line handsomely as he came trotting up in the rear guard Todd fell into line upon the left and Quantrell gave the word. The Federal pursuit had hardly time to fire a volley before it was rent into shreds and scattered upon the prairie.

ORDER NUMBER 11, AUGUST, 1863

TWO days after his safe arrival in Missouri from the Lawrence massacre, Quantrell disbanded the Guerrillas. Fully six thousand Federals were on his track. The savageness of the blow struck there had appalled and infuriated the country. The journalistic pulse of the North rose to fever heat and beat as though to its raging fever there had been added raving insanity. In the delirium of the governing powers impossible things were demanded. Quantrell was to be hunted to the death; he was to be hanged, drawn and quartered; his band was to be annihilated; he was to be fought with fire, persecution, depopulation and wholesale destruction. At the height of the very worst of these terrible paroxysms, Ewing's famous General Order No. 11 was issued. It required every citizen of Jackson, Cass, Bates and a portion of Vernon counties to abandon their houses and come either into the lines of designated places that were fortified, or within the jurisdiction of said lines. If neither was done, and said citizens remained outside beyond the time limit specified for such removal, they were to be regarded as outlaws and punished accordingly. Innocent and guilty alike felt the rigors of this unprecedented proscription. For the Union man there was the same line of demarkation that was drawn for the secessionist. Age had no immunity; sex was not regarded. The rights of property vanished; predatory bands preyed at will; nothing could be sold; everything had to be abandoned; it was the obliterating of prosperity by counties; it was the depopulation of miles upon miles of fertile territory in a night.

General Ewing had been unjustly censured for the promulgation of such an order and held responsible in many ways for its execution. The genius of a celebrated painter, Captain George C. Bingham of Missouri, had been evoked to give infamy to the vandalism of the dead and voice to the indignation of history over its consummation. Bingham's picture of burning and plundering houses, of a sky made awful with mingling flames and smoke, of a long line of helpless fugitives going away they knew not whither, of appealing women and gray haired non-combatants, of skeleton chimneys rising like wrathful and accusing things from the wreck of pillaged homesteads, of uniformed things called officers rummaging in trunks and drawers, of colonels loaded with plunder, and captains gaudy in stolen jewelry, will live longer than the memories of the strife, and keep alive horrible memories long after Guerrilla and Jayhawker are well forgotten.

Ewing, however, was a soldier. General Order No. 11 came from district headquarters at St. Louis where Scofield commanded, and through Scofield from Washington City direct. Ewing had neither choice nor discretion in the matter. He was a brave, conscientious, hard fighting officer who did his duty as it came to his hands to do. He could not have made, if he had tried, one hair of the infamous Order white or black. It was a portion of the extraordinary order of things, and Ewing occupied towards it scarcely the attitude of an instrument. He promulgated it but he did not originate it; he gave it voice but he did not give it form and substance; his name had been linked to it as to something that should justly cause shame and reproach, but history in the end will separate the soldier from the man and render unto the garb of the civilian what it has failed to concede to the uniform of the commander. As a citizen of the republic he deplored the cruelty of an enactment which he knew to be monstrous; but as a soldier in the line of duty, the necessity of the situation could not justify a moment's argument. He had but to obey and to execute, and he did both—and mercifully.

For nearly three weeks Jackson County was a Pandemonium, together with the counties of Cass, Bates, Vernon, Clay and Lafayette. Six thousand Federals were in the saddle, but Quantrell held his grip upon these counties despite everything. Depopulation was going on in a two-fold sense—one by emigration or exodus, and one by the skillful killing of perpetual ambushment and lyings-in-waiting. In detachments of ten, the Guerrillas divided up and fought everywhere. Scattered, they came together as if by instinct. Driven from the flanks of one column, they appeared in the rear of another. They had voices that were as the voices of the night birds. Mysterious horsemen appeared on all the roads. Not a single Federal scouting or exploring party escaped paying toll. Sometimes the aggregate of the day's dead was simply enormous. Frequently the assailants were never seen. Of a sudden, and rising, as it were, out of the ground, they delivered a deadly blow and rode away in the darkness—invisible.

FIGHTS AND SKIRMISHES DURING FALL AND WINTER, 1863–1864

AS the Lawrence raid put the whole Federal forces after us, it was a continuous fight from September 1, 1863, to Price's raid in August, 1864, but Quantrell held his own.

Up to the time of the Lawrence massacre there had been no scalping done; after it a good deal. Abe Haller, brother of Lieutenant William Haller, was wounded and hiding in some timber near Texas Prairie in the eastern edge of Jackson County. Alone, he faced seventy-two men, killing and wounding five of the attacking party, when he fell. His slayers scalped him and cut off his ears. Shortly afterwards Andy Blunt came upon the body, mutilated as it was, and pointed out the marks of the knife to his companions.

"We have something to learn yet, boys," he said, "and we have learned it." "Scalp for scalp hereafter!"

The next day Blunt, Long, Clemens, Bill Anderson and McGuire captured four militiamen from a regiment belonging to North Missouri. Blunt scalped each of the four, leaving their ears intact, however. He said he had no use for them.

FIRE PRAIRIE

The killing went on. Between Fire Prairie and Napoleon Gregg, Taylor, Nolan, Little and Frank James captured six of Pennick's militiamen. They held over them a kind of court martial and killed them all. These were not scalped.

WELLINGTON

The next day Richard Kenney, John Farretts, Jesse James and Sim Whitsett attacked a picket post of eight men about a mile from Wellington and annihilated it, cutting them off from the town and running them in a contrary direction. Not a man escaped.

LEXINGTON ROAD

Two days afterwards Ben Morrow, Pat O'Donald and Frank James ambushed an entire Federal company between Salem church on the Lexington road and Widow Child's. They fought eighty men for nearly an hour, killing seven and wounding thirteen. O'Donald was wounded three times and James and Morrow each once slightly.

SHAWNEE TOWN ROAD

Todd gathered together thirty of his old men and, getting a volunteer guide who knew every hog path in the country, went around past Kansas City boldly and took up a position on the Shawnee Town road, looking for a train of wagons bringing infantry into Kansas City. There were twenty wagons with twenty soldiers to the wagon, besides the drivers. Here and there between the wagons intervals of fifty yards had been permitted to grow. Todd waited until all the wagons but three had passed by the point of his ambush when he sprang out upon them and poured into them and upon their jammed and crowded freight a deadly rain of bullets. Every shot told. Todd butchered sixty in the three wagons and turned away from his work of death and pursued the balance.

INDEPENDENCE

Cole Younger, while Todd was operating in Kansas, gathered about him ten men and hid himself as close to Independence as it was possible to get without getting into town. His eyes for some time had been fastened upon a large corral. He sent William Hulse out to reconnoiter the position and bring word of the guard stationed to protect it. Younger avoided the pickets and by eleven o'clock had made the distance, halting at the turning off place on the main road and giving his horses in charge of two of the detachment. With the other eight on foot led by Hulse, he crept close to the reserve post and fired point blank into the sleeping guard, some rolled up in their blankets and some resting at ease about the fire. Choosing his way as well as possible by the uncertain light. Younger escaped unpursued with three excellent horses to the man after killing seventeen Federals in the night attack and wounding many more.

BLUE SPRINGS FIGHT IN DECEMBER, 1863

COLONEL PENNICK'S men came from Independence down to Blue Springs and burned houses, killed old men—too old to be in the service. They numbered two hundred, while Quantrell's men numbered one hundred. On the road from Blue Springs to Independence they killed John Sanders and a man named Kimberland—both old men—and left them lying in the roadway. If neighbors had not offered their services the hogs would have eaten their bodies. They burned from two to twelve houses and left the families homeless.

The people of the neighborhood sent a runner to Quantrell. We mounted, struck a gallop and did not slow down until we charged the rear and went through them like fire through stubble, killing as we went. After the battle was over we counted seventy-five killed and an equal number wounded. Those who were not hit were so scared that we had no more trouble with them.

On our retreat Quantrell's password was, "Bat them, boys, over the left eye."

A good old citizen by the name of Uncle George Rider, hearing the firing and seeing us coming, got off his horse and laid down in the woods close to the road, face up, having a belly on him like a ten-gallon beer keg. Quantrell said to Dick Burns, "You go out and bat him over the left eye." Burns went out to him and hollered back to Quantrell that "he has been dead a week; see how he is swelled up." We had lots of fun afterwards about his belly saving him.

WELLINGTON

FOUR miles east of Wellington stood a large house occupied by some lewd women, notorious for their favors and their enticements. Poole knew the situation well, and suggested to Jarrette that a sufficient detour should be made to encompass the building. Arriving there about eleven o'clock at night, it appeared from the outside as if there were some kind of a frolic. Lights shone from many of the windows, music and the sound of dancing feet could be heard occasionally. Frank James crept to a back door and looked in and counted five women and eleven men. Some of the men were sitting on the laps of the women and some were so close to others that to risk a volley would be murderous. At no time without hitting a woman could they make sure of hitting a man. They waited an hour to gain a favorable opportunity, but waited in vain. Jarrette solved the problem.

He was dressed in Federal uniform, and after placing his men so as to cut off any escape from the house if the occupants once came outside, he rode boldly up to the fence in front of the premises and cried, "Hello!" A soldier came to the door with a gun in his hand and answered him. Jarrette continued, "Who are you that you come to this place in defiance of every order issued for a month? What business have you here tonight? Who gave you permission to come? Where are your passes? Come out here and let me read them." Thinking Jarrette a provost captain scouting for runaways from the Lexington garrison, ten of the eleven militiamen started confidently for the fence, receiving, when half way, the crushing fire of twenty concealed Guerrillas. In a space four blankets might have covered the ten fell and died, only one of the lot discharging a weapon or making a pretense of resistance.

Frank James stooped to count them, and as he rose he remarked: "There are but ten here. Awhile ago there were eleven." The building was entered, searched from top to bottom in every nook and corner, but no soldier. The women were questioned, one at a time, separately. They knew only that when the man at the fence called they all went out together.

Frank James, whose passive face had from the first expressed neither curiosity nor doubt, spoke up again and briefly: "Awhile ago I counted but five women, now there are six." Save four sentinels on duty at either end of the main road, Guerrillas had gathered together in the lower large room of the dwelling house. The fire had burned low, and was fitful and flickering. Where there had been half a dozen candles there were now only two.

"Bring more," said Poole, "and we will separate this wolf from the ewes."

"Aye, if we have to strip the lot," spoke up a coarse voice in the crowd.

"Silence," cried Jarrette, laying a hand upon a pistol and turning to his men in the shadow, "not a woman shall be touched. We are wild beasts, yes, but we war on wild beasts."

More light was brought, and with a candle in each hand Poole went from woman to woman, scanning the face of each long and searchingly, and saying when he had finished, "I give it up. If one of the six here is a man, let him keep his dress and his scalp."

Frank James, just behind Poole, had inspected each countenance also as the candles passed before it, and when Poole had done speaking, he laid a finger upon a woman's shoulder and spoke as one having authority: "This is the man. If I miss my reckoning, shoot me dead."

The marvelous nerve, which up to this time had stood with the militiaman as a shield and a defense, deserted him when the extremity came, and he turned ghastly white, trembled to his feet, and fell, sobbing and praying on his knees. Horrified by the slaughter in the yard, and afraid to rush from the house lest he be shot down also, he hurriedly put on the garments of one of the women, composed his features as best he could, and waited in suspense the departure of the Guerrillas. Almost a boy, his smooth face was fresher and fairer than the face of any real woman there. His hair, worn naturally long and inclined to be brown, was thick and fine. The dress hid his feet, or the boots would have betrayed him at the start. Not knowing that an observation had been made before the firing, and the number accurately taken of both men and women, he hoped to brave it through and laugh afterwards and tell to his messmates how near death had passed by him and did not stop. The reaction, however, upon discovery, was pitiful. He was too young to die, he pleaded. He had never harmed a human being in his life. If he was spared he would abandon the army and throw away his gun. As he prayed he wept, but Jarrette abated further abasement of his manhood.

"He is yours, James," he said, "and fairly yours. When he changed color ever so little under Poole's inspection you saw it and no other man saw it, and he belongs to you. Take him." Property in human flesh was often disposed of in this way.

"Come," said Frank James, lifting the young Federal up to his feet with his left hand and drawing his revolver with his right; "come outside, it is not far to go."

Scarcely able to stand, yet unresisting, the militiaman followed the Guerrilla—the lamb following the tiger. As they went by the ghastly heap, all ragged and intangible in the uncertain light, the one shuddered and the other was glad. At the fence the poor prisoner was so weak he could scarcely climb it. Beyond the fence was the road and down this road a few hundred yards towards Lexington Frank James led his victim. Under the shadows of a huge tree he halted. It was quite dark there. Only the good God could see what was done; the leaves shut the stars out.

"Do not kill me for my mother's sake," came from the pinched lips of the poor victim, "for I have no one else to pray for me. Spare me just this once."

"You are free," said James, "go," and as he spoke he pointed in the direction of Lexington.

"Free? You do not kill me? You tell me go? Great God, am I sleeping or awake!" and the man's teeth chattered and he shook as if in a fit of ague.

"Yes, go and go quickly; you are past the guards, past all danger; you belong to me and I give you your life. **Go!**"

At that moment Frank James lifted his pistol in the air and fired. When he returned to the house Jarrette, who had heard the pistol shot, rallied him.

"Yes," he said, "it was soon over. Boys and babies are not hard to kill." James had just taken the trouble to save the life of a Federal soldier because he had appealed to him in the name of his mother.

Jarrette continued on his raid. South of Lexington six miles he came suddenly upon nine Federals in a school house, sheltered against a heavy rain that was falling. After shooting the nine and appropriating the house, he propped each corpse up to a desk, put a book before it and wrote upon the blackboard fixed against the wall: "John Jarrette and David Poole taught this school today for one hour. We found the pupils all loyal and we left them as we found them."

Again in the German settlement a company of militia were engaged and cut to pieces. Near Dover five militiamen from Carroll County were caught encamped at Tebo bridge and shot. Near Waverly ten men at odd times were picked up and put out of the way. And on the return march to Jackson County no less than forty-three straggling Federals, in squads of from three to nine, were either surprised or overtaken and executed without trial or discussion.

THE GRINTER FIGHT

A DUTCH colonel, with his company of men, one day came into Piser's saloon in Independence, Mo., and got to drinking pretty freely and said to Piser, the saloon keeper:

"Dose you'se knows where dot Quantrell, dot kill-devil, iss? Gife us another drink. We are going out and get dot Quantrells today, brings his scalps in on ours vidle bits."

Piser, a friend of both Federals and Confederates, pleaded with him to leave the job alone. The Dutch colonel wore a pair of earrings as big as a ring in a bull's nose.

"Give us another drinks," the Dutch colonel said. "Ills tells youse we are going after Quantrells, and ven I finds him I is going to says, 'Haltz!' and ven I says 'haltz' dot means him stops a little viles."

So they took the Independence and Harrisonville road and found Quantrell camped close to old man Grinter's and as usual always ready for any surprise, for he had been surprised so much. When the Dutch colonel and his company came in sight, Quantrell ordered his men to mount and charge, which they did, and when the smoke cleared away only two remained to tell the story. They were a couple hundred yards away sitting on their horses cursing us, calling us all kinds of d— —d "secesh," telling us to come on. I said to Sim Whitsett, "Let's give them a little chase. They seem to be so brave." We took after them but they would not stand. They broke and ran. We ran them for a quarter of a mile down the big road. One fell off his horse dead, the other one jumped off and ran into old man Grinter's house. Mrs. Grinter was in the yard. He ran to her and said, "Hide me." She put him under a bee gum. Sim and I stopped but never could find him. Sim does not to this day like the Grinter name. Sim said, "I got the earring, but he is the lad." He afterwards gave them to a girl on Texas Prairie, Missouri. Poor old Dutchman. He lost his life with all his men but one.

TAKING DINNER WITH THE FEDERALS

THE CENTRALIA MASSACRE

IN history, this is called a battle of massacre, but there never was a fight during the Civil War that was fought any more fairly than this battle was fought.

Along about September, 1864, at Paris, in Monroe County, there had been a Federal garrison three hundred strong, under the command of a Major Johnson. These soldiers, on the watch for Anderson, had been busy in scouting expeditions and had come down as near to Centralia as Sturgeon.

After Anderson had done all the devilment that he could lay his hands to in Centralia and had retired again to the Singleton camp, Major Johnson came into the pillaged town, swearing all kind of fearful and frightful things.

At the head of his column a black flag was carried. So also was there one at the head of Todd's column. In Johnson's ranks the Stars and Stripes for this day had been laid aside. In the ranks of the Guerrillas the Stars and Stripes flew fair and free, as if there had been the intention to add to the desperation of the sable banner the gracefulness and abandon of legitimate war.

The Union citizens of Centralia, knowing Anderson only in his transactions, besought Johnson to beware of him. He was no match for Anderson. It was useless to sacrifice both himself and his men. Anderson had not retreated; he was in ambush somewhere about the prairie. He would swoop down like an eagle; he would smite and spare not. Johnson was as brave as the best of them, but he did not know what he was doing. He had never in his life fought Guerrillas—such Guerrillas as were now to meet him.

He listened patiently to the warnings that were well meant, and he put away firmly the hands that were lifted to stay his horse. He pointed gleefully to his black flag, and boasted that quarter should neither be given nor asked. He had come to carry back with him the body of Bill Anderson, and that body he would have, dead or alive.

Fate, however, had not yet entirely turned its face away from the Federal officer. As he rode out from the town at the head of his column a young Union girl, described as very fair and beautiful, rushed up to Major Johnson and halted him. She spoke as one inspired. She declared that a presentiment had come to her, and that if he led his men that day against Bill Anderson, she felt and knew that but few of them would return alive. The girl almost knelt in the dust as she besought the leader, but to no avail.

Johnson's blood was all on fire, and he would march and fight, no matter whether death waited for him one mile off, or one hundred miles off. He not only carried a black flag himself, and swore to give no quarter, but he declared on his return that he would devastate the country and leave of the habitations of the southern men not one stone upon another. He was greatly enraged towards the last. He cursed the people as "damned secesh," and swore that they were in league with the murderers and robbers. Extermination, in fact, was what they all needed, and if fortune favored him in the fight, it was extermination that all should have. Fortune did not favor him.

Johnson rode east of south, probably three miles. The scouts who went to Singleton's barn, where Anderson camped, came back to say that the Guerrillas had been there, had fed there, had rested there, and had gone down into the timber beyond to hide themselves. It was now about four o'clock in the afternoon.

Back from the barn, a long, high ridge lifted itself up from the undulating level of the more regular country and broke the vision southward. Beyond this ridge a wide, smooth prairie stretched itself out, and still beyond this prairie, and further to the south, was the timber in which the scouts said Bill Anderson was hiding.

As Johnson rode towards the ridge, still distant from it a mile or so, ten men anticipated him by coming up fair to view, and in skirmishing order. The leader of this little band, Captain John Thrailkill, had picked for the occasion David and John Poole, Frank and Jesse James, Tuck Hill, Peyton Long, Ben Morrow, James Younger, E. P. DeHart, Ed Greenwood and Harrison Trow. Next to Thrailkill rode Jesse James, and next to Jesse, Frank. Johnson had need to beware of what might be before him in the unknown when such giants as these began to show themselves.

The Guerrillas numbered, all told, exactly two hundred and sixty-two. In Anderson's company there were sixty-one men, in George Todd's forty-eight, in Poole's forty-nine, in Thomas Todd's fifty-four, and in Thrailkill's fifty—two hundred and sixty-two against three hundred.

As Thrailkill went forward to skirmish with the advancing enemy, Todd came out of the timber where he had been hiding, and formed a line of battle in an old field in front of it. Still further to the front a sloping hill, half a mile away, arose between Johnson and the Guerillas. Todd rode to the crest of this, pushing Thrailkill well forward into the prairie beyond, and took his position there. When he lifted his hat and waved it the whole force was to move rapidly on. Anderson held the right, George Todd joined to Anderson, Poole to George Todd, Thomas Todd to Poole, and Thrailkill to Thomas Todd—and thus were the ranks arrayed.

The ten skirmishers quickly surmounted the hill and disappeared. Todd, as a carved statue, stood his horse upon its summit. Johnson moved right onward. Some shots at long range were fired and some bullets from the muskets of the Federals reached to and beyond the ridge where Todd watched, Peyton Long by his side. From a column of fours Johnson's men galloped at once into line of battle, right in front, and marched so, pressing up well and calmly.

The advanced Guerillas opened fire briskly at last, and the skirmishing grew suddenly hot. Thrailkill, however, knew his business too well to tarry long at such work, and fell back towards the ridge.

As this movement was being executed, Johnson's men raised a shout and dashed forward together and in a compact mass order formation, ranks all gone. This looked bad. Such sudden exultation over a skirmish wherein none were killed exhibited nervousness. Such a spontaneous giving way of the body, even beyond the will of their commander, should have manifested neither surprise nor delight and looked ominous for discipline.

Thrailkill formed again when he reached Todd's line of battle, and Johnson rearranged his ranks and went towards the slope at a brisk walk. Some upon the right broke into a trot, but he halted them, cursed them, and bade them look better to their line.

Up the hill's crest, however, a column of men suddenly rode into view, halted, dismounted and seemed to be busy or confused about something.

Inexperienced, Johnson is declared to have said to his adjutant: "They will fight on foot—what does that mean?" It meant that the men were tightening their saddle girths, putting fresh caps on their revolvers, looking well to bridle reins and bridle bits, and preparing for a charge that would have about it the fury of a whirlwind. By and by the Guerrillas were mounted again. From a column they transformed themselves into a line two deep and with a double interval between all files. At a slow walk they moved over the crest towards Major Johnson, now advancing at a walk that was more brisk.

Perhaps it was now five o'clock. The September sun was low in the west, not red nor angry, but an Indian summer sun, full yet of generous warmth and grateful beaming. The crisp grass crinkled under foot. A distance of five hundred yards separated the two lines. Not a shot had been fired. Todd showed a naked front, bare of skirmishers and stripped for a fight that he knew would be murderous to the Federals. And why should they not stand? The black flag waved alike over each, and from the lips of the leaders of each there had been all that day only threats of extermination and death.

Johnson halted his men and rode along his front speaking a few calm and collected words. They could not be heard in Todd's ranks, but they might have been divined. Most battle speeches are the same. They abound in good advice. They are generally full of such sentences as this: "Aim low, keep cool, fire when you get loaded. Let the wounded lie till the fight is over."

But could it be possible that Johnson meant to receive the charge of the Guerrillas at a halt! What cavalry books had he read? Who had taught him such ruinous and suicidal tactics? And yet, monstrous as the resolution was in a military sense, it had actually been made, and Johnson called out loud enough to be heard by the opposing force: "Come on, we are ready for the fight!"

The challenge was accepted. The Guerillas gathered themselves together as if by a sudden impulse, and took the bridle reins between their teeth. In the hands of each man there was a deadly revolver. There were carbines, too, and yet they had never been unslung. The sun was not high, and there was great need to finish quickly whatever had need to be done. Riding the best and fastest horses in Missouri, George Shepherd, Oll Shepherd, Frank Shepherd, Frank Gregg, Morrow,

McGuire, Allen Parmer, Hence and Lafe Privin, James Younger, Press Webb, Babe Hudspeth, Dick Burnes, Ambrose and Thomas Maxwell, Richard Kinney, Si and Ike Flannery, Jesse and Frank James, David Poole; John Poole, Ed Greenwood, Al Scott, Frank Gray, George Maddox, Dick Maddox, De Hart, Jeff Emery, Bill Anderson, Tuck Hill, James Cummings, John Rupe, Silas King, James Corum, Moses Huffaker, Ben Broomfield, Peyton Long, Jack Southerland, William Reynolds, William and Charles Stewart, Bud Pence, Nat Tigue, Gooly Robertson, Hiram Guess, Buster Parr, William Gaw, Chat Rennick, Henry Porter, Arch and Henry Clements, Jesse Hamlet, John Thrailkill, Si Gordon, George Todd, Thomas Todd, William and Hugh Archie, Plunk Murray, Ling Litten, Joshua Esters, Sam Wade, Creth Creek, Theodore Castle, John Chatman and three score men of other unnamed heroes struck fast the Federal ranks as if the rush was a rush of tigers. Frank James, riding a splendid race mare, led by half a length, then Arch Clements, then Ben Morrow, then Peyton Long and then Harrison Trow.

There was neither trot not gallop. The Guerrillas simply dashed from a walk into a full run. The attack was a hurricane. Johnson's command fired one volley and not a gun thereafter. It scarcely stood until the five hundred yards were passed over. Johnson cried out to his men to fight to the death, but they did not wait even to hear him through. Some broke ranks as soon as they had fired, and fled. Others were attempting to reload their muskets when the Guerrillas, firing right and left, hurled themselves upon them. Johnson fell among the first. Mounted as described, Frank James singled out the leader of the Federals. He did not know him then. No words were spoken between the two. When James had reached within five feet of Johnson's position, he put out a pistol suddenly and sent a bullet through his brain. Johnson threw out his hands as if trying to reach something above his head and pitched forward heavily, a corpse. There was no quarter. Many begged for mercy on their knees. The Guerrillas heeded the prayer as a wolf might the bleating of a lamb. The wild route broke up near Sturgeon, the implacable pursuit, vengeful as hate, thundering in the rear. Death did its work in twos, threes, in squads—singly. Beyond the first volley not a single Guerrilla was hurt, but in this volley Frank Shepherd, Hank Williams and young Peyton were killed, and Richard Kenney mortally wounded. Thomas Maxwell and Harrison Carter were also slightly wounded by the same volley, and two horses were killed, one under Dave Poole and one under Harrison Trow. Shepherd, a giant in size, and brave as the best in a command where all are brave, fought the good fight and died in the harness. Hank Williams, only a short time before, had deserted from the Federals and joined Poole, giving rare evidences, in his brief Guerrilla career, of great enterprise and consummate daring. Peyton was but a beardless boy from Howard County, who in his first battle after becoming a Guerrilla, was shot dead.

Probably sixty of Johnson's command gained their horses before the fierce wave of the charge broke over them, and these were pursued by five Guerrillas—Ben Morrow, Frank James, Peyton Long, Arch Clements and Harrison Trow—for six miles at a dead run. Of the sixty, fifty-two were killed on the road from Centralia to Sturgeon. Todd drew up the command and watched the chase go on. For three miles nothing obstructed the vision. Side by side over the level prairie the five stretched away like the wind, gaining step by step and bound by bound, upon the rearmost rider. Then little puffs of smoke rose. No sounds could be heard, but dashing ahead from the white spurts terrified steeds ran riderless.

Knight and Sturgeon ended the killing. Five men had shot down fifty-two. Arch Clements, in apportionment made afterwards, had credited to himself fourteen. Trow ten, Peyton Long nine, Ben Morrow eight, Frank James, besides killing Major Johnson and others in the charge upon the dismounted troopers, killed in the chase an additional eleven.

Johnson's loss was two hundred ninety one. Out of the three hundred, only nine escaped.

History has chosen to call the ferocious killing at Centralia a butchery. In civil war, encounters are not called butcheries where the combatants are man to man and where over either ranks there waves a black flag.

Johnson's overthrow, probably, was a decree of fate. He rushed upon it as if impelled by a power stronger than himself. He did not know how to command and his men did not know how to fight. He had, by the sheer force of circumstances, been brought face to face with two hundred and sixty-two of the most terrible revolver fighters the American war or any other war ever produced; and he deliberately tied his hands by the very act of dismounting, and stood in the shambles until he was shot down. Abject and pitiable cowardice matched itself against recklessness and desperation, and the end could be only just what the end was. The Guerrillas did unto the militia just what the militia would have done unto them if fate had reversed the decision and given to Johnson what it permitted to Todd.

ANDERSON

IN June, 1864, Anderson crossed the Missouri River. Four miles out from the crossing place, he encountered twenty-five Federals, routed them at the first onset, killing eight, two of whom Arch Clements scalped, hanging the ghastly trophies at the head-stall of his bridle. One of the two scalped was a captain and the commander of the squad.

Killing as he marched, Anderson moved from Carroll into Howard, entered Huntsville the last of June with twenty-five men, took from the county treasury $30,000, and disbanded for a few days for purposes of recruiting.

The first act of the next foray was an ambuscade into which Anderson fell headlong. Forty militia waylaid him as he rode through a stretch of heavy bottom land, filled his left shoulder full of turkey shot, killed two of his men and wounded three others. Hurt as he was, he charged the brush, killing eighteen of his assailants, captured every horse and followed the flying remnant as far as a single fugitive could be tracked through the tangled undergrowth.

In July Anderson took Arch Clements, John Maupin, Tuck and Woot Hill, Hiram Guess, Jesse Hamlet, William Reynolds, Polk Helms, Cave Wyatt and Ben Broomfield and moved up into Clay County to form a junction with Fletch Taylor. By ones and twos he killed twenty-five militiamen on the march and was taking breakfast at a house in Carroll County when thirty-eight Federals fired upon him through doors and windows, the balls knocking dishes onto the floor and playing havoc with chinaware and eatables generally. The Guerrillas, used to every phase of desperate warfare, routed their assailants after a crashing volley or two, and held the field, or rather the house. In the melee Anderson accidentally shot a lady in the shoulder, inflicting a painful wound, and John Maupin killed the captain commanding the scouts, cut off his head and stuck it upon a gate-post to shrivel and blacken in the sun.

In Ray County, one hundred and fifty Federal cavalrymen found Andersons' trail, followed it all day, and just at nightfall struck hard and viciously at the Guerrillas. Anderson would not be driven without a fight. He charged their advance guard, killed fourteen out of sixty, and drove the guard back upon the main body. Clements, Woot Hill, Hamlet and Hiram Guess had their horses killed and were left afoot in the night to shift for themselves. Walking to the Missouri River, ten miles distant, and fashioning a rude raft from the logs and withes, Hamlet crossed to Jackson County and made his way safe into the camp of Todd.

While with Anderson John Coger was wounded again in the right leg. Suffering from this wound and with another one in the left shoulder, he had been carried by his comrades to a house close to Big Creek, in Cass County, and when it was night, and by no road that was generally traveled. Coger, without a wound of some kind or in some portion of his body, would have appeared as unaccountable to the Guerrillas as a revolver without a mainspring.

At the end of every battle some one reckless fighter asked of another: "Of course, John can't be killed, but where is he hit this time?" And Coger, himself, no matter how often or how badly hurt, scarcely ever waited for a old wound to get well before he was in the front again looking for a new one. He lived for fifty years after the battle, carrying thirteen bullet wounds.

The wonderful nerve of the man saved him many times during the war in open and desperate conflicts, but never when the outlook was so unpromising as it was now, with the chances as fifty to one against him.

Despite his two hurts, Coger would dress himself every day and hobble about the house, watching all the roads for the Federals. His pistols were kept under the bolster of his bed.

One day a scout of sixty militiamen approached the house so suddenly that Coger had barely time to undress and hurry to bed, dragging in with him his clothes, his boots, his tell-tale shirt and his four revolvers. Without the help of the lady of the house he surely would have been lost. To save him she surely—well, she did not tell the truth.

The sick man lying there was her husband, weak from a fever. Bottles were ostentatiously displayed for the occasion. At intervals Coger groaned and ground his teeth, the brave, true woman standing close to his bedside, wiping his brow every now and then and putting some kind of smelling stuff to his lips.

A Federal soldier, perhaps a bit of a doctor, felt Coger's left wrist, held it awhile, shook his head, and murmured seriously: "A bad case, madam, a bad case, indeed. Most likely pneumonia."

Coger groaned again.

"Are you in pain, dear?" the ostensible wife tenderly inquired.

"Dreadful!" and a spasm of agony shot over the bushwhacker's sun-burnt face.

For nearly an hour the Federal soldiers came and went and looked upon the sick man moaning in his bed, as deadly a Guerrilla as ever mounted a horse or fired a pistol.

Once the would-be doctor skirted the edge of the precipice so closely that if he had stepped a step further he would have pitched headlong into the abyss. He insisted upon making a minute examination of Coger's lungs and laid a hand upon the coverlet to uncover the patient. Coger held his breath hard and felt upward for a revolver. The first inspection would have ruined him. Nothing could have explained the ugly, ragged wound in the left shoulder, nor the older and not entirely healed one in the right leg. The iron man, however, did not wince. He neither made protest nor yielded acquiescence. He meant to kill the doctor, kill as many more as he could while life lasted and his pistol balls held out, and be carried from the room, when he was carried at all, feet foremost and limp as a lock of hair. Happily a woman's wit saved him. She pushed away the doctor's hand from the coverlet and gave as the emphatic order of her family physician that the sick man should not be disturbed until his return.

Etiquette saved John Coger, for it was so unprofessional for one physician to interfere with another physician's patient, and the Federal soldier left the room and afterwards the house.

PRESS WEBB, A BORN SCOUT

PRESS WEBB was a born scout crossed upon a highlander. He had the eyes of an eagle and the endurance of the red deer. He first taught himself coolness, and then he taught it to others. In traveling he did not travel twice the same road. Many more were like him in this—so practicing the same kind of woodcraft and cunning—until the enemy began to say: "That man Quantrell has a thousand eyes."

Press Webb was ordered to take with him one day Sim Whitsett, George Maddox, Harrison Trow and Noah Webster and hide himself anywhere in the vicinity of Kansas City that would give him a good view of the main roads leading east, and a reasonably accurate insight into the comings and going of the Federal troops.

The weather was very cold. Some snow had fallen the week before and melted, and the ground was frozen again until all over the country the ground was glazed with ice and traveling was made well nigh impossible. The Guerrillas, however, prepared themselves and their horses well for the expedition. Other cavalrymen were forced to remain comparatively inactive, but Quantrell's men were coming and going daily and killing here and there.

On the march to his field of operation, Webb overtook two Kansas infantrymen five miles west of Independence on the old Independence road. The load under which each soldier staggered proved that their foraging expedition had been successful. One had a goose, two turkeys, a sack of dried apples, some yarn socks, a basket full of eggs and the half of a cheese; while the other, more powerful or more greedy than the first—toiled slowly homeward, carrying carefully over the slippery highway a huge bag miscellaneously filled with butter, sausages, roasted and unroasted coffee, the head of a recently killed hog, some wheaten biscuits not remarkably well cooked, more cheese and probably a peck of green Jenniton apples. As Webb and his four men rode up the foragers halted and set their loads on the ground as if to rest. Piled about them, each load was about as large as a forager.

Webb remarked that they were not armed and inquired of the nearest forager—him with the dried apples—why he ventured so far from headquarters without his gun.

"There is no need of a gun," was the reply, "because the fighting rebels are all out of the country and the stay-at-homes are all subjugated. What we want we take, and we generally want a good deal."

"A blind man might see that," Webb rather grimly replied, "but suppose some of Quantrell's cut-throats were to ride up to you as we have done, stop to talk with you as we have done, draw out a pistol as I am doing this minute, cover you thus, and bid you surrender now as I do, you infernal thief and son of a thief, what would you say then?"

"Say!"—and the look of simple surprise yet cool indifference which came to the Jayhawker's face was the strongest feature of the tragedy—"what could I say but that you are the cut-throat and I am the victim? Caught fairly, I can understand the balance. Be quick."

Then the Jayhawker rose up from the midst of his spoils with a sort of quiet dignity, lifted his hat as if to let his brow feel the north wind, and faced without a tremor the pistol which covered him.

"I cannot kill you so," Webb faltered, "nor do I know whether I can kill you at all. We must take a vote first."

Then to himself: "To shoot an unarmed man, and a brave man at that, is awful."

There amid the sausages and cheese, the turkeys and the coffee grains, the dried apples and the green, five men sat down in judgment upon two. Whitsett held the hat; Webster fashioned the ballots. No arguments were had. The five self-appointed jurors were five among Quantrell's best and bravest. In extremity they had always stood forth ready to fight to the death; in the way of killing they had done their share. The two Kansas Jayhawkers came close together as if in the final summing up they might find in the mere act of dying together some solace. One by one the Guerrillas put into the hat of Whitsett a piece of paper upon which was written his vote. All had voted. Harrison Trow drew forth the ballots silently. As he unfolded the first and read from it deliberately; "Death," the younger Jayhawker blanched to his chin and put a hand on the shoulder of his comrade. The two listened to the count, with every human faculty roused and abnormally impressionable. Should any one not understanding the scene pass, they would not be able to comprehend the situation—one man standing bareheaded, solemnly, and all the eyes bent keenly forward as another man drew from a hat a dirty slip of folded paper and read therefrom something that was short like a monosyllable and sepulchral like a shroud.

"Life," said the second ballot, and "Life" said the third. The fourth was for death and made a tie. Something like the beating of a strong man's heart might have been heard, and something as though a brave man were breathing painfully through his teeth lest a sigh escape him. Whitsett cried out: "One more ballot yet to be opened. Let it tell the tale, Trow, and make an end to this thing speedily." Trow, with scarcely any more emotion than a surgeon has when he probes a bullet wound, unfolded the remaining slip of paper, and read, "Life"!

The younger Jayhawker fell upon his knees and the elder ejaculated solemnly: "Thank God, how glad my wife will be."

Webb breathed as one from whose breast a great load had been lifted and put back into its scabbard his revolver. The verdict surprised him all the more because it was so totally unexpected, and yet the two men there—Jayhawkers though they were and loaded with spoils of plundered farm houses—were as free to go as the north wind that blew or the stream that was running by.

As they rode away the Guerrillas did not even suggest to one another the virtue of the parole. At the two extremities of their peculiar warfare there was either life or death. Having chosen deliberately as between the two, no middle ground was known to them.

Press Webb approached to within sight of Kansas City from the old Independence road, made a complete circle about the place, as difficult as the traveling was, entered Westport notwithstanding the presence of a garrison there; heard many things told of the plans and number of the Federal forces upon the border; passed down between the Kansas river and what is now known as West Kansas City, killed three foragers and captured two six-mule wagons near the site of the present gas works; gathered up five head of excellent horses, and concealed himself for two days in the Blue Bottom, watching a somewhat notorious bawdy house much frequented by Federal soldiers. This kind of houses during the war, and when located upon dangerous or debatable grounds, were man traps of more or less sinister histories.

Eleven women belonged to this bagnio proper, but on the night Webb stalked it and struck it, there had come five additional inmates from other quarters equally as disreputable. Altogether the male attendants numbered twenty, two lieutenants, one sergeant major, a corporal, four citizens and twelve privates from an Iowa regiment. Webb's attacking column, not much larger than a yard stick, was composed of the original detail, four besides himself.

The night was dark; the nearest timber to the house was two hundred and fifty yards. There was ice on everything. The tramping of iron shod feet over the frozen earth reverberated as artillery wheels. At the timber line Maddox suggested that one man should be left in charge of the horses, but Webb overruled the point.

"No man shall stir tonight," he argued, "except he be hunted for either war or women. The horses are safe here. Let us dismount and make them fast."

As they crept to the house in single file, a huge dog went at Harrison Trow as if he would not be denied, and barked so furiously and made so many other extravagant manifestations of rage, that a man and a woman came to the door of the house and bade the dog devour the disturber. Thus encouraged he leaped full at Trow's throat and Trow shot him dead.

In a moment the house emptied itself of its male occupants, who explored the darkness, found the dog with the bullet through its head, searched everywhere for the author of the act, and saw no man, nor heard any retreating steps, and so returned unsatisfied to the house, yet returned, which was a great deal.

As for the Guerrillas, as soon as Trow found himself obliged to shoot or be throttled, they rushed back safely and noiselessly to their horses, mounted them and waited. A pistol shot, unless explained, is always sinister to soldiers. It is not to be denied. Fighting men never fire at nothing. This is a maxim not indigenous to the brush, nor an outcome of the philosophy of those who were there. A pistol shot says in so many words: "Something is coming, is creeping, is crawling, is about—look out!"

The Federals heard this one—just as pertinent and as intelligible as any that was ever fired—but they failed to interpret aright this significant language of the ambuscade, and they suffered accordingly.

Webb waited an hour in the cold, listening. No voices were heard, no skirmishers approached his position, no scouts from the house hunted further away than the lights from the windows shone, no alarm had been raised, and he dismounted with his men and again approached the house.

By this time it was well on to twelve o'clock. Chickens were crowing in every direction. The north wind had risen high and was blowing as a winter wind always blows when there are shelterless men abroad in a winter night.

The house, a rickety frame house, was two stories high, with two windows on the north and two on the south.

George Maddox looked in at one of these windows and counted fourteen men, some well advanced in liquor and some sober and silent and confidential with the women. None were vigilant. The six upstairs were neither seen nor counted.

At first it was difficult to proceed upon a plan of action. All the Federals were armed, and twenty armed men holding a house against five are generally apt, whatever else may happen, to get the best of the fighting.

"We cannot fire through the windows," said Webb, "for women are in the way."

"Certainly" replied Whitsett, "we do not war upon women."

"We cannot get the drop on them," added Trow, "because we cannot get to them."

"True again," replied Maddox, "but I have an idea which will simplify matters amazingly. On the south there is a stable half full of plank and plunder. It will burn like pitch pine. The wind is from the north is strong, and it will blow away all danger from the house. Were it otherwise I would fight against the torch, for not even a badger should be turned out of its hole tonight on word of mine, much less a lot of women. See for yourself and say if the plan suits you."

They saw, endorsed the proposition, and put a match at once to the hay and to the bundles of fodder. Before the fire had increased perceptibly the five men warmed their hands and laughed. They were getting the frost out of their fingers to shoot well, they said. A delicate trigger touch is necessary to a dead shot.

"Fire!"

All of a sudden there was a great flare of flames, a shriek from the women and a shout from the men. The north wind drove full head upon the stable, roared as like some great wild beast in pain.

The Federals rushed to the rescue. Not all caught up their arms as they hurried out—not all even were dressed.

PRESS WEBB, A BORN SCOUT

The women looked from the doors and windows of the dwelling, and thus made certain the killing that followed. Beyond the glare of the burning outhouse, and massed behind a fence fifty paces to the right of the consuming stable, the Guerrillas fired five deadly volleys into the surprised and terrified mass before them, and they scattered, panic-striken and cut to pieces,—the remnant frantically regained the sheltering mansion.

Eight were killed where they stood about the fire; two were mortally wounded and died afterwards; one, wounded and disabled, quit the service; five, severely or slightly wounded, recovered; and four, unhurt, reported that night in Kansas City that Quantrell had attacked them with two hundred men, and had been driven off, hurt and badly worsted, after three-quarters of an hour's fight. Press Webb and his four men did what work was done in less than five minutes.

LITTLE BLUE

CAPTAIN DICK YAGER, commanding ten men, the usual number the Guerrillas then operated with, engaged twenty Federals under Lieutenant Blackstone of the Missouri Militia regiments, and slew fourteen.

Yager had ambushed a little above a ford over the Little Blue and hid behind some rocks about fifteen feet above the crossing place, and Blackstone, unconscious of danger, rode with his troops leisurely into the water and halted midway in the stream that his horses might drink. He had a tin cup tied to his saddle and a bottle of whiskey in one of his pockets. After having drunk and while bending over from his stirrups to dip the cup into the water, a volley hit him and knocked him off his horse dead, thirteen others falling close to and about him at the same time.

Jarrette and Poole, each commanding ten men, made a dash into Lafayette County and struck some blows to the right and left, which resounded throughout the West.

Poole pushed into the German settlement and comparatively surprised them.

Where Concordia now is, there was then a store and a fort, strong and well built. This day, however, Poole came upon them unawares and found many who properly belonged to the militia feeding stock and in an exposed position. Fifteen of these he killed and ten he wounded severely but not so severely as to prevent them from making their way back to the fort.

ARROCK FIGHT, SPRING OF 1864

TODD and Dave Poole went east through Fayette County to Saline County and thence to Arrock, with one hundred and twenty men to avenge the death of Jim Janes, Charles Bochman and Perkins, who were captured by the Federals under Captain Sims.

The men who captured the boys made them dig their own graves and shot them and rolled them into them. We made the raid for the benefit of this captain and were successful. We caught him and his men playing marbles in the street, unaware of any danger. We rode slowly into town with our Federal uniforms on, Sim Whitsett in advance.

"Boys," said he, "I will knock the middle man out for you."

He fired the first shot. Then it was a continuous fire and the Federals surrendered in a very few minutes.

We killed twenty-five men, wounded thirty-five and had only one man, Dick Yager, wounded.

Ben Morrow and I had the pleasure of capturing the captain in an upstairs bed room of a hotel. He died with quick consumption with a bullet through his head.

We captured one hundred and fifty men and swore them out of service.

FIRE BOTTOM PRAIRIE FIGHT, SPRING OF 1864

ONE of the most daring things I ever witnessed was when Ben Morrow saved my life at the time they got me off my horse at the battle of Fire Prairie Creek near Napoleon, Missouri, in the spring of 1864.

George Todd, in command, was sent out to meet a bunch of Federals going from Lexington to Independence. We expected to meet them in the road and charge them in the usual way, but they got word we were coming and dismounted, hid their horses in the woods and came up, on foot, and fired on us from the brush as we charged. They caught my horse by the bridle and before they could shoot me I jumped off over the horse's head. As I went over, I fired at the man holding him and he fell. I was on foot amidst the worst of them. This gave me an advantage as I could fire in any direction I wanted to and they could not, as their men were all around me and in danger of being hit by their own bullets. I saw a hole where a large tree had been uprooted, a hole large enough to conceal me almost, and I made direct for it, firing at everything in sight as I went.

Captain Todd ordered his men back, with three of them, Babe Hudspath, Bill McGuire and Tid Sanders, so badly wounded they were unable to go further.

I was left there in the hole, bullets blowing up the dirt all around me, the hole being deep enough for me to get out of sight. I lay on my back, loading my pistols and watched close as a hawk. They said I was dead and wanted to come up and get my pistols. Whenever one would show his head I took a shot at him and they saw that I was very much alive and their scheme would not work.

One of the blue billies climbed a tree close by, thinking he would be able to get a better shot at me. I waited until he got fairly up in the tree and then shot him in the thigh and down he came. I kept up firing, thinking the boys would hear it and come back and help me.

They were a quarter of a mile off when Ben Morrow said, "Boys, we are all here except Harrison Trow, and do you hear that shooting? He is still alive and by G—d I am going back to get him." So on came Ben Morrow, yelling and shooting with a pistol in each hand. When within forty yards of me and letting in on the enemy with a pistol in each hand, he saw me and came straight for me. I caught the crupper of his saddle, jumped up behind him, and pulling two pistols, one in each hand, firing as we went, we got safely away. From that day on, I would have died any where, and any place and any how for Ben Morrow, who saved my life at the risk of his own.

After the Fayette fight Lieutenant Jim Little, one of Quantrell's best men, was badly wounded in Howard County, Missouri, and Quantrell went with him to the woods to take care of him until he recovered.

Then, after the Centralia fight, Ben Morrow, Bill Hulsh and I went to where Quantrell and Jim Little were in the woods. Jim was much better by this time, so that Quantrell could leave him and he came back to us in Jackson County, where we swam the river on our horses near Saline City. After we had crossed the river we went to a house to get breakfast and dry our clothes. Quantrell wanted to intercept General Price who was on a raid and have a consultation with him.

At this house we discovered some Federal clothing—caps, etc.—in the hall and asked whose they were. We were told they belonged to some Federal soldiers who had stayed there through the night and attended a dance. We captured them at once and swore them out of service. We then went on to intercept Price at Waverly, Saline County, Missouri, where arrangements were made for Quantrell's men to take the advance clear on up through Fayette and Jackson Counties, and up through Kansas City. We were in advance all of the way from that time until Price started south, and we went with him, about one hundred miles, almost to the Arkansas line, and turned back to Jackson County.

DEATH OF TODD AND ANDERSON, OCTOBER, 1864

CURTIS' heavy division, retreating before General Price all the way from Lexington to Independence, held the western bank of the Little Blue, and some heavy stone walls and fences beyond. Marmaduke and Shelby broke his hold from these, and pressed him rapidly back to and through Independence, the two Colorado regiments covering his rear stubbornly and well. Side by side McCoy and Todd had made several brilliant charges during the morning, and had driven before them with great dash and spirit every Colorado squadron halted to resist the continual marching forward of the Confederate cavalry.

Ere the pursuit ended for the day, half of the 2nd Colorado regiment drew up on the crest of a bold hill and made a gallant fight. Their major, Smith, a brave and dashing officer, was killed there, and there Todd fell. General Shelby, as was his wont, was well up with the advance, and leading recklessly the two companies of Todd and McCoy. Next to Shelby's right rode Todd and upon his left was McCoy. Close to these and near to the front files were Colonels Nichols, Thrailkill, Ben Morrow, Ike Flannery and Jesse James.

The trot had deepened into a gallop, and all the crowd of skirmishers covering the head of the rushing column were at it, fierce and hot, when the 2nd Colorado swept the road with a furious volley, broke away from the strong position held by them and hurried on through the streets of Independence, followed by the untiring McCoy, as lank as a fox-hound and as eager.

That volley killed Todd. A Spencer rifle ball entered his neck in front, passed through and out near the spine, and paralyzed him. Dying as he fell, he was yet tenderly taken up and carried to the house of Mrs. Burns, in Independence. Articulating with great difficulty and leaving now and then almost incoherent messages to favorite comrade or friend, he lingered for two hours insensible to pain, and died at last as a Roman.

George Todd was a Scotchman born, his father holding an honorable position in the British navy. Destined also for the sea, it was the misfortune of the son to become engaged in a personal difficulty in his eighteenth year and kill the man with whom he quarreled. He fled to Canada, and from Canada to the United States. His father soon after resigned and followed him, and when the war began both were railroad contractors in North Missouri, standing well with everybody for business energy, capacity and integrity.

Todd made a name by exceeding desperation. His features presented nothing that could attract attention. There was no sign in visible characters of the powers that was in him. They were calm always, and in repose a little stern; but if anything that indicated "a look of destiny" was sought for, it was not to be found in the face of George Todd. His was simple and confiding, and a circumspect regard for his word made him a very true but sometimes a very blunt man. In his eyes the fittest person to command a Guerrilla was he who inspired the enemy before people began to say: "That man, George Todd, is a tiger. He fights always; he is not happy unless he is fighting. He will either be killed soon or he will do a great amount of killing." It has just been seen that he was not to be killed until October, 1864—a three years' lease of life for that desperate Guerrilla work never had a counterpart. By and by the Guerrillas themselves felt confidence in such a name, reliance in such an arm, favor for such a face. It was sufficient for Todd to order a march to be implicitly followed; to plan an expedition to have it immediately carried out; to indicate a spot on which to assemble to cause an organization sometimes widely scattered or dispersed to come together as the jaws of a steel trap.

Nature gave him the restlessness of a born cavalryman and the exterior and the power of voice necessary to the leader of desperate men. Coolness, and great activity were his main attributes as a commander. Always more ready to strike than to speak, if he talked at all it was only after a combat had been had, and then modestly. His conviction was the part he played, and he sustained with unflinching courage and unflagging energy that which he had set down for his hands to do.

A splendid pistol shot, fearless as a horseman, knowing nature well enough to choose desperate men and ambitious men, reticent, heroic beyond the conception of most conservative people, and covered with blood as he was to his brow, his fall was yet majestic, because it was accompanied by patriotism.

Before the evacuation of Independence, Todd was buried by his men in the cemetery there, and Poole succeeded to the command of his company, leading it splendidly.

The night they buried Todd, Ike Flannery, Dick Burns, Andy McGuire, Ben Morrow, Press Webb, Harrison Trow, Lafe Privin, George Shepherd, George Maddox, Allen Parmer, Dan Vaughn, Jess and Frank James and John Ross took a solemn oath by the open grave of the dead man to avenge his death, and for the following three days of incessant battle it was remarkable how desperately they fought—and how long.

Until General Price started southward from Mine Creek in full retreat, the Guerrillas under Poole remained with him, scouting and picketing, and fighting with the advance. After Mine Creek they returned to Bone Hill, in Jackson County, some going afterwards to Kentucky with Quantrell, and some to Texas with George Shepherd.

Henceforward the history of the Guerrillas of Missouri must be the history of detachments and isolated squads, fighting always, but fighting without coherency or other desire than to kill.

Anderson had joined Price at Boonville and the meeting was a memorable one. The bridles of the horses the men rode were adorned with scalps. One huge red-bearded Guerrilla—six feet and over, and girdled about the waist with an armory of revolvers—had dangling from every conceivable angle a profuse array of these ghastly trophies. Ben Price was shocked at such evidence of a warfare so utterly repugnant to a commander of his known generosity and forbearance, and he ordered sternly that they be thrown away at once. He questioned Anderson Long of Missouri, of the forces in the state, of the temper of the people, of the nature of Guerrilla warfare, of its relative advantages and disadvantages and then when he had heard all he blessed the Guerrillas probably with about as much unction as Balaam blessed Israel.

General Price was a merciful man. Equable in every relation of life, conservative by nature and largely tolerant through his earlier political training, thousands are alive today solely because none of the harsher or crueler indulgences of the Civil War were permitted to the troops commanded by this conscientious officer.

Finally, however, he ordered Anderson back into North Missouri, and he crossed at Boonville upon his last career of leave taking, desperation and death.

Tired of tearing up railroad tracks, cutting down telegraph poles, destroying miles and miles of wire, burning depots, and picking up and killing isolated militiamen, terrified at the uprising in favor of Price, Anderson dashed into Danville, Montgomery County, where sixty Federals were stationed in houses and strong places.

He had but fifty-seven men, and the fight was close and hot.

Gooley Robinson, one of his best soldiers, was mortally wounded while exposing himself in a most reckless manner.

It was difficult to get the enemy out of the houses. Snatching up torches and braving the guns of the entrenched Federals, Dick and Ike Berry put fire to one house. Arch Clements and Dick West to another, Theo. Castle, John Maupin and Mose Huffaker to a third, and Ben Broomfield, Tuck, Tom and Woot Hill to the fourth.

It was a night of terror and agony. As the militiamen ran out they were shot down by the Guerrillas in the shadow. Some wounded, burnt to death, and others, stifled by the heat and smoke, rushed, gasping and blackened into the air, to be riddled with bullets. Eight, barely, of the garrison escaped the holocaust.

Anderson turned west towards Kansas City, expecting to overtake General Price there. En route he killed as he rode. Scarcely an hour of all the long march was barren of a victim. Union men, militiamen, Federal soldiers, home guards, Germans on general principles—no matter what the class or the organization—if they were pro-United States, they were killed.

Later on, in the month of October, while well advanced in Ray County, Anderson received the first news of the death of Todd and the retreat of Price. By this time, however, he had recruited his own command to several hundred, and had joined to it a detachment of regular Confederates, guiding and guarding to the South a motley aggregation of recruits, old and young. Halting one day to rest and to prepare for a passage across the Missouri River, close to Missouri City, Anderson found one thousand Federals—eight hundred infantry and two hundred cavalry. He made haste to attack them. His young lieutenant, Arch Clements, advised him urgently against the attack, as did Captain A. E. Asbury, a young and gallant Confederate officer, who was in company with him, commanding fifty recruits. Others of his associates did the same, notably Colonel John Holt, a Confederate officer, and Colonel James H. R. Condiff. Captain Asbury was a cool, brave, wary man who had had large experience in border fighting, and who knew that for a desperate charge raw recruits could not be depended upon.

Anderson would not be held back. Ordering a charge, his horse ran away with him and he was seventy-five yards ahead of his followers when he was killed. Next to him was William Smith, a veteran Guerrilla of four years' service. Five balls struck him, and three struck Anderson. Next to Smith was John Maupin, who was wounded twice, and next to Maupin, Cundill, who was also hit, and next to Cundill, Asbury, who got four bullets through his clothes. John Holt, Jim Crow Chiles and Peyton Long had their horses killed. The three Hill brothers and Dick West and ten others of Anderson's old company fought their way up to Anderson's body and sought to bring it out. Tuck Hill was shot, so was his brother Woot and Dick West. Their wounds were severe, but not mortal. Once they succeeded in placing it upon a horse; the horse was killed and fell upon the corpse and held it to the ground. Still struggling heroically over the body of his idolized commander, Hank Patterson fell dead, not a foot from the dead Guerrilla. Next, Simmons was killed, and then Anson Tolliver, and then Paul Debonhorst, and then Smith Jobson, and then Luckett, then John McIlvaine, and finally Jasper Moody and William Tarkington. Nothing could live before the fire of the concealed infantry and the Spencer carbines of the cavalry.

A single blanket might have covered the terrible heap of dead and wounded who fought to recover all that remained of that tiger of the jungle. John Pringle, the red-headed giant of the Boonville scalps, far ahead of his company, was the last man killed, struggling even to the death to bear back the corpse. He was a captain of a company, and a veteran of the Mexican war, but he did what he would not order his men to do—he rushed up to the corpse heap and fastened about the leg of Anderson a lariat that he might drag the body away. The Federals killed his horse. Shot once, he tugged at the rope himself, bleeding pitifully. Shot again, he fell, struggled up to his feet, fired every barrel of three revolvers into the enemy, and received as a counter blow two more bullets.

This time he did not rise again or stir, or make a moan. All the wild boar blood in his veins had been poured out, and the bronzed face, from being rigid, had become august.

Joseph and Arch Nicholson, William James, Clell Miller and John Warren, all young recruits in their first battle, fought savagely in the melee, and all were wounded. Miller, among those who strove to rescue the corpse of Anderson, was shot, and Warren, wounded four times, crawled back from the slaughter pen with difficulty. A minie ball had found the heart of Anderson. Life, thank God, was gone when a rope was put around his neck and his body dragged as the body of a dog slain in the woods.

Many a picture was taken of the dead lion, with his great flowing beard, and that indescribable pallor of death on his bronzed face. The Federals cut his head off and stuck it on a telegraph pole.

GOING SOUTH, FALL OF 1864

TODD'S death fell upon the spirits of his men as a sudden bereavement upon the hearts of a happy and devoted family. Those who mourned for him mourned all the more tenderly because they could not weep. Nature, having denied to them the consolation of tears, left them the infinite intercourse and remembrances of comradeship and soldierly affection.

The old bands, however, were breaking up. Lieutenant George Shepherd, taking with him Matt Wyman, John Maupin, Theo. Castle, Jack Rupe, Silas King, James and Alfred Corum, Bud Story, Perry Smith, Jack Williams, Jesse James and Arthur Devers, Press Webb, John Norfolk and others to the number of twenty-six, started south to Texas, on the 13th of November, 1864. With Shepherd also were William Gregg and wife, Richard Maddox and wife, and James Hendrix and wife. These ladies were just as brave and just as devoted and just as intrepid in peril or extremity as were the men who marched with them to guard them.

Jesse and Frank James separated at White River, Arkansas, Frank to go to Kentucky with Quantrell, and Jesse to follow the remnant of Todd's still organized veterans into Texas.

Besides killing isolated squads of Federals and making way for every individual militiaman who supposed that the roads were absolutely safe for travelers because General Price and his army had long been gone, Shepherd's fighting for several days was only fun. On the 22nd, however, Captain Emmett Goss, an old acquaintance of the Fifteenth Kansas Cavalry, Jennison's, was encountered, commanding thirty-two Jayhawkers.

Of late Goss had been varying his orgies somewhat. He would drink to excess and lavish his plunder and money on ill-famed mistresses, who were sometimes Indians, sometimes negresses, and but rarely pure white. He was about thirty-five years old, square built, had broad shoulders, a swaggering gait, stood six feet when at himself, and erect, had red hair and a bad eye and a face that meant fight when cornered—and desperate fight at that.

November 22, 1864, was an autumn day full of sunshine and falling leaves. Riding southward from Missouri Lieutenant Shepherd met Captain Goss riding northward from Cane Hill. Shepherd had twenty-six men, rank and file. It was an accidental meeting—one of those sudden, forlorn, isolated, murderous meetings not rare during the war—a meeting of outlying detachments that asked no quarter and gave none. It took place on Cabin Creek, in the Cherokee Nation. Each rank arrayed itself speedily. There were twenty-six men against thirty-two. The odds were not great—indeed they never had been considered at all. There came a charge and a sudden and terrible storm of revolver bullets.

Nothing so weak as the Kansas detachment could possibly live before the deadly prowess and pistol practice of the Missourians. Of the thirty-two, twenty-nine were killed. One, riding a magnificent race horse, escaped on the wings of the wind—one, a negro barber, was taken along to wait upon the Guerrillas, and the third, a poor emaciated skeleton, as good as dead of consumption, was permitted to ride on northward, bearing the story of the thunderbolt.

Among the Missourians four were killed. In the melee Jesse James encountered Goss and singled him out from all the rest. As James bore down upon him, he found that his horse, an extremely high-spirited and powerful one, had taken the bit in its teeth and was perfectly unmanageable. Besides, his left arm being left weak from a scarcely healed wound, it was impossible for him to control his horse or even to guide him.

Pistol balls were as plentiful as the leaves that were pattering down. However, James had to put up his revolver as he rode, and rely upon his right hand to reinforce his left. Before he could turn his horse and break its hold upon his bit, Goss had fired upon him four times. Close upon him at last James shot him through and through. Goss swayed heavily in his saddle, but held on.

"Will you surrender?" Jesse asked, recocking his pistol and presenting it again.

"Never," was the stern reply. Goss, still reeling in the saddle and bleeding dreadfully.

When the blue white smoke curled up again there was a riderless steed among the trees and a guilty spirit somewhere out in the darkness of the unknown. It took two dragoon revolver bullets to finish this one, and yet James was not satisfied with his work.

There was a preacher along who also had sat himself steadfast in the saddle, and had fought as the best of them did. James rode straight at him after he had finished Goss. The parson's heart failed him at last, however, and he started to run. James gained upon him at every step. When close enough for a shot, he called out to him:

"Turn about like a man, that I may not shoot you in the back." The Jayhawker turned, and his face was white and his tongue voluble.

"Don't shoot me," he pleaded, "I am the chaplain of the Thirteenth Kansas; my name is U. P. Gardner, I have killed no man, but have prayed for many; spare me." James did not answer. Perhaps he turned away his head a little as he drew out his revolver. When the smoke lifted, Gardner was dead upon the crisp sere grass with a bullet through his brain.

Maddox, in this fight, killed three of Goss' men, Gregg five, Press Webb three, Wayman four, Hendrix three, and others one or two each.

The march through the Indian country was one long stretch of ambushments and skirmishes.

Wayman stirred up a hornet's nest one afternoon, and though stung twice himself quite severely, he killed four Indians in single combat and wounded the fifth who escaped.

Press Webb, hunting the same day for a horse, was ambushed by three Pins and wounded slightly in the arm. He charged singlehanded into the brush and was shot again before he got out of it, but he killed the three Indians and captured three excellent ponies, veritably a god-send to all.

The next day about noon the rear guard, composed of Jesse James, Bud Story, Harrison Trow and Jack Rupe, was savagely attacked by seventy-five Federal Cherokees and driven back upon the main body rapidly. Shepherd, one of the quickest and keenest soldiers the war produced, had formed every man of the command in the rear of an open field through which the enemy must advance and over which in return a telling charge could be made. The three heroic women, mounted on excellent horses and given shelter in some timber still further to the rear of the Guerrilla line, bade their husbands, as they kissed them, fight to the death or conquer. The Indians bore down as if they meant to ride down a regiment. Firing their pistols into their very faces with deadly effect, the rear guard had not succeeded in stopping them a single second, but when in the counter-charge Shepherd dashed at the oncoming line, it melted away as snow in a thaw. Shepherd, Maddox, Gregg, the two Corums, Rupe, Story, James, Hendrick, Webb, Smith Commons, Castle, Wayman and King fought like men who wanted to make a clean and a merciless sweep.

John Maupin, not yet well from the two ugly wounds received the day Anderson was killed, insisted on riding in the charge, and was shot the third time by the Indian into whom he had put two bullets and whose horse he rushed up to secure.

Jesse James had his horse killed and a pistol shot from his hand. Several other Guerrillas were wounded but none killed, and Williams, James Corum and Maddox lost horses.

Of the sixty-five Indians, fifty-two were counted killed, while some, known to be wounded, dragged themselves off into the mountain and escaped.

During the battle Dick Maddox's wife could not keep still under cover, and commenced to shoot at the enemy, and had a lock of her hair shot off just above the ear.

THE SURRENDER

EARLY in the month of March, 1865, Captain Clements, having been reinforced by ten men under the command of Captain David Poole, marched from Sherman, Texas, to Mount Pleasant, Titus County, Arkansas. From Mount Pleasant, on the 14th of April, the march began once more and for the last time into Missouri. Forming an advance of David Poole, John Poole, John Maupin, Jack Bishop, Theo. Castle, Jesse James and Press Webb, Clements pushed on rapidly, killing five militiamen in one squad, ten in another, here and there a single one, and now and then as many together as twenty. In Benton County, Missouri, a Federal militiaman named Harkness, was captured, who had halted a brother of Clements and burnt the house of his mother. James, Maupin and Castle held Harkness tightly while Clements cut his throat and afterwards scalped him.

At Kingsville, in Johnson County, something of a skirmish took place and ten Federals were killed. A militiaman named Duncan, who had a bad name locally and who was described as being a highwayman and a house burner, also was captured at the same time. Being fifty-five years of age and gray headed did not save him. But before he surrendered he fought a desperate battle. Knowing instinctively what his fate would be if he fell alive into the hands of any hostile organization, much less a Guerrilla organization, he took a stand behind a plank fence, armed with a Spencer rifle and two revolvers, and faced the enemy, now close upon him. Arch Clements, Jesse James and Jack Bishop dashed at Duncan. The first shot killed his horse, and in falling the horse fell upon the rider. At the second fire Clement's horse also was killed, but James stopped neither for the deadly aim of the old man nor for the help of his comrades who were coming up as fast as they could on foot. He shot him three times before he knocked him from his feet to his knees, but the fourth shot, striking him fair in the middle of the forehead, finished the old man and all his sins together.

The last of April a council was held among the Guerrillas to discuss the pros and cons of a surrender. Virtually the war was over. Everywhere the regular Confederate armies had surrendered and disbanded, and in no direction could any evidences be discovered of that Guerrilla warfare which many predicted would succeed to the war of the regular army and the general order. All decided to do as the rest of the Southern forces had done.

Anxious, however, to give to those of the command who preferred a contrary course the dignity and the formality of official authority, Captain Clements entered Lexington, Mo., on the fifteenth, with Jesse James, Jess Hamlet, Jack Rupe, Willis King and John Vanmeter, bearing a flag of truce. The provost marshall of

Lexington, Major J. B. Rogers, was a liberal officer of the old regime, who understood in its fullest and broadest sense that the war was over, and that however cruel or desperate certain organizations or certain bodies of men had been in the past, all proscription of them ceased with their surrender.

Shortly after the surrender, and as Jesse James was riding at the head of a column with the white flag, eight Federals were met who were drunk and who did not see the flag of truce or did not regard it. They fired point blank at the Guerrillas, and were charged in turn and routed with the loss of four killed and two wounded. These eight men were the advance of a larger party of sixty, thirty Johnson County militia, and thirty of the Second Wisconsin Cavalry. These in the counter attack drove back the Guerrillas and followed them fiercely, especially the Second Wisconsin. Vanmeter's horse was killed but Jack Rupe stopped under fire for him and carried him to safety. James and Clements, although riding jaded horses—the same horses, in fact, which had made the long inhospitable trip up from Texas—galloped steadily away in retreat side by side, and fighting as best they could. Mounted on a superb black horse, a single Wisconsin trooper dashed ahead of the balance and closed in swiftly upon James, who halted to court the encounter. At a distance of ten feet both fired simultaneously and when the smoke cleared away the brave Wisconsin man was dead with a dragoon ball through his heart. Scarcely had this combat closed before another Wisconsin trooper rushed at James, firing rapidly, and closing in as he fired. James killed his horse, and the Federal in turn sent a bullet through James' right lung. Then the rush passed over and past him. Another volley killed his horse, and as the Johnson County militia galloped by, five fired at him as he lay bleeding under the prostrate horse.

Clements, seeing horse and rider going down together, believed his beloved comrade was killed, and strove thereafter to make good his own escape.

Extricating himself with infinite toil and pain, Jesse James left the road for the woods, pursued by five Federals, who fired at him constantly as they followed. At a distance of two hundred yards he killed the foremost Federal and halted long enough under fire to disencumber himself of his heavy cavalry boots, one of which was a quarter full of blood. He fired again and shattered the pistol arm of the second pursuer, the other three closing up and pressing the maimed Guerrilla as ravenous hounds the torn flanks of a crippled stag. James was getting weaker and weaker. The foremost of the three pursuers could be heard distinctly yelling: "Oh! g——d——n your little soul, we have you at last! Stop, and be killed like a gentleman!"

James did not reply, but when he attempted to lift his trusty dragoon pistol to halt the nearest trooper, he found it too heavy for his hand. But reinforcing his right arm with his left, he fired finally at the Wisconsin man almost upon him and killed him in the saddle.

Perhaps then and there might have been an end made to the career of the desperate Guerrilla if the two remaining pursuers had been Wisconsin Cavalry instead of Johnson County militia; but terrified at the prowess of one who had been so terribly wounded, and who killed even as he reeled along, the militiamen abandoned the chase and James, staggering on four or five hundred yards further, fell upon the edge of a creek and fainted. From the 15th to the 17th he lay alongside the water, bathing his wound continually and drinking vast quantities of water to quench his burning thirst and fever. Towards sunset, on the evening of the 17th, he crawled to a field where a man was plowing, who proved to be a Southern man and a friend.

That night he rode fifteen miles to the house of a Mr. Bowman, held upon a horse by his new-found friend, where he remained, waited upon by Clements and Rupe, until the surrender of Poole, on the 21st, with one hundred and twenty-nine Guerrillas.

Major Rogers was so well satisfied that James would die that he thought it unnecessary to parole him, and so declared. To give him every chance, however, for his life, and to enable him to reach his mother, then a fugitive in Nebraska, Rodgers furnished him with transportation, money and a pass.

A good many of my men surrendered with Poole, while others planned to go to Old Mexico with me and not surrender at all. However, when I came up from the South, planning to go back to Old Mexico and join General Shelby with his old command, some of my best citizen friends insisted on my surrendering and going home, and through their influence arrangements were made with Major Rodgers to meet me at the Dillard farm, on Texas Prairie. There we held a consultation, he and I, for about half a day, regarding my surrender. He promised me protection and my side arms, and the horse that I had, and I surrendered, receiving the protection he had promised me.

I went home and went to work and took my part in trying to make peace with the Federal soldiers, some of whom proved to be very good friends to me, and we lived very peacefully after the war.

I very much opposed and tried to put a stop to the robbery, thieving and horse stealing that was so prominent after the war, and advised the boys that got into trouble to leave the country time and time again, and go to Old Mexico while it was yet time to get away.

I returned home with no money and no means at all, but found plenty of friends who were ready to help me and who furnished me money to start with.

I advise all who read this book to appreciate character above money.

DEATH OF QUANTRELL

QUANTRELL, with forty-eight of the most daring of his old band, accompanied Shepherd as far south as White River, Arkansas. He left them there to go to his old home in Maryland. He passed all Federal camps, had no trouble staying in Federal camps, eating with Federal soldiers, playing Federal himself until he reached Upton Station, in Hart County, Kentucky, where he crossed the Louisiana & Nashville Railroad, still representing himself and his men as Federal soldiers.

Near Marion County he entered the Lebanon and Campbellville turnpike at Rolling Fork and traveled north to New Market, thence east to Bradford, and from Bradford towards Hustonville, camping for the night preceding the entrance into this place at Major Dray's, on Rolling Fork. Thirty Federal soldiers were at garrison at Hustonville, possessed of as many horses in splendid condition, and these Quantrell determined to appropriate. No opposition was made to his entrance into the town. No one imagined him to be other than a Union officer on a scout.

He dismounted quietly at a hotel in the place and entered at once into a pleasant conversation with the commander of the post. Authorized by their chieftain, however, to remount themselves as speedily as possible and as thoroughly as possible, the Guerrillas spread quickly over the town in search for horses, appropriating first what could be found in the public stables and later on those that were still needed to supply the deficiency, from private places.

As Quantrell conversed with the commander, a Federal private made haste to inform him of the kind of work the newcomers were doing, and to complain loudly of the unwarranted and outrageous appropriation.

Enraged and excited, the commander snatched up a brace of revolvers as he left his headquarters and buckled them about him and hurried to the nearest livery stable where the best among the animals of his men had been kept. Just as he arrived, Allen Parmer was riding out mounted on a splendid horse. The Federal major laid hands upon the bridle and bade Parmer dismount. It was as the grappling of a wave with a rock.

No Guerrilla in the service of the South was cooler or deadlier; none less given to the emotion of fear. He looked at the Federal major a little curiously when he first barred the passageway of his horse and even smiled pleasantly as he took the trouble to explain to him the nature of the instructions under which he was operating.

"D——n you and d——n your instructions," the major replied fiercely. "Dismount!"

"Ah," ejaculated Parmer, "has it really come to this?" and then the two men began to draw. Unquestionably there could be but one result. The right hand of the Federal major had hardly reached the flap of his revolver, before Parmer's pistol was against his forehead, and Parmer's bullet had torn half the top of his head off.

In June, 1865, Quantrell started from Bedford Russell's, in Nelson County, with John Ross, William Hulse, Payne Jones, Clark Hockinsmith, Isaac Hall, Richard Glasscock, Robert Hall, Bud Spence, Allen Parmer, Dave Helton and Lee McMurtry. His destination was Salt River.

At Newel McClaskey's the turnpike was gained and traveled several miles, when a singularly severe and penetrating rain storm began. Quantrell, to escape this, turned from the road on the left and into a woods pasture near a postoffice called Smiley. Through this pasture and for half a mile further he rode until he reached the residence of a Mr. Wakefield, in whose barn the Guerrillas took shelter. Unsuspicious of danger and of the belief that the nearest enemy was at least twenty miles away, the men dismounted, unbridled their horses, and fed them at the racks ranged about the shed embracing two sides of the barn.

While the horses were eating the Guerrillas amused themselves with a sham battle, choosing sides and using corncobs for ammunition. In the midst of much hilarity and boisterousness, Glasscock's keen eye saw through the blinding rain a column of cavalry, one hundred and twenty strong, approaching the barn at a trot.

He cried out instantly, and loud enough to be heard at Wakefield's house sixty yards away: "Here they are! Here they are." Instantly all the men were in motion and rushing to their horses.

Captain Edward Terrell, known well to Quantrell and fought stubbornly once before, had been traveling the turnpike from the direction of Taylorsville, as completely ignorant of Quantrell's proximity as Quantrell had been of his, and would have passed on undoubtedly without a combat if the trail left by the Guerrillas in passing from the road to the pasture had not attracted attention. This he followed to within sight of the barn, understood in a moment the character of the men sheltered there, and closed upon it rapidly, firing as he came on.

Before a single Guerrilla had put a bridle upon a horse, Terrill was at the main gate of the lot, a distance of some fifty feet from the barn, and pouring such a storm of carbine bullets among them that their horses ran furiously about the lot, difficult to approach and impossible to restrain.

Fighting desperately and deliberately, and driving away from the main gate a dozen or more Federals stationed there, John Ross, William Hulse, Allen Parmer, Lee McMurtry, and Bud Pence, cut their way through, mounted and defiant. The entire combat did not last ten minutes. It was a fight in which every man had to do for himself and do what was done speedily.

Once above the rattling of musketry, the neighing of horses and the shouting of combatants, Quantrell's voice rang out loud and clear: "Cut through, boys, cut through somehow! Don't surrender while there is a chance to get out."

The fire upon the Guerrillas was furious. Quantrell's horse, a thoroughbred animal of great spirit and speed, could not be caught. His master, anxious to secure him, followed him composedly about the lot for several minutes, trying under showers of bullets to get hands upon his favorite.

At this moment Clark Hockingsmith, who was mounted and free to go away at a run, saw the peril of his chief, and galloped to his rescue. Quantrell, touched by this act of devotion, recognized it by a smile, and held out his hand to his comrade without speaking. Hockingsmith dismounted until Quantrell took his own place in the saddle, and then sprang up behind him.

Another furious volley from Terrill's men lining all the fence about the great gate, killed Hockingsmith and killed the horse he and Quantrell were upon. The second hero now gave his life to Quantrell. Richard Glasscock also had secured his own horse as Hockingsmith had done and was free to ride' away in safety as he had been.

Opposite the main entrance to the barn lot there was an exit uncovered by the enemy and beyond this exit a stretch of heavy timber. Those who gained the timber were safe. Hockingsmith knew it when he deliberately laid down his life for his chief, and Glasscock knew it when he also turned about and hurried up to the two men struggling there—Quantrell to drag himself out from under the horse and Hockingsmith in the agonies of death.

The second volley from the gate mortally wounded Quantrell and killed Glasscock's horse. Then a charge of fifty shouting, shooting men swept over the barn lot. Robert Hall, Payne Jones, David Helton, and Isaac Hall had gone out some time before on foot. J. B. Tooley, A. B. Southwick and C. H. Southwick, wounded badly, escaped fighting. Only the dead man lying by his wounded chief, and Glasscock, erect, splendid, and fighting to the last, remained as trophies of the desperate combat. Two balls struck Quantrell. The first, the heavy ball of a Spencer carbine, entered close to the right collar bone, ranged down along the spine, injuring it severely, and hid itself somewhere in the body. The second ball cut off the finger next to the little finger of the left hand, tearing it from its socket, and lacerating the hand itself badly. The shoulder wound did its work, however, for it was a mortal wound. All the lower portion of Quantrell's body was paralyzed and as he was lifted and carried to Wakefield's house his legs were limp and his extremities cold and totally without sensation.

At no time did he either make complaint or moan. His wonderful endurance remained unimpaired to the end. His mind, always clear in danger, seemed to recognize that his last battle had been fought and his last encounter finished. He talked very little. Terrill came to him and asked if there was any good service he might do that would be acceptable.

"Yes," said Quantrell quietly, "have Clark Hockingsmith buried like a soldier."

After he had been carried to the house of Wakefield and deposited upon a pallet, he spoke once more to Terrell:

"While I live let me stay here. It is useless to haul a dying man about in a wagon, jolting out what little life there is left in him."

Terrell pledged his word that he should not be removed, and rode away in pursuit of those who had escaped.

Some of the fugitive Guerrillas soon reached the well known rendezvous at the house of Alexander Sayers, twenty-three miles from Wakefield's, with tidings of the fight.

Frank James heard the story through with a set face, strangely white and sorrowful, and then he arose and cried out: "Volunteers to go back. Who will follow me to see our chief, living or dead?"

"I will go back," said Allen Parmer, "and I," said John Ross, and "I," said William Hulse.

"Let us ride, then," rejoined James, and in twenty minutes more—John Ross having exchanged his jaded horse for a fresh one—these four devoted men were galloping away to Wakefield's.

At two o'clock in the morning they were there. Frank James dismounted and knocked low upon the door. There was the trailing of a woman's garments, the circumspect tread of a watching woman's feet, the noiseless work of a woman's hand upon the latch and Mrs. Wakefield, cool and courtly, bade the strange armed men upon the threshold to enter.

Just across on the other side of the room from the door a man lay on a trundle bed. James stood over the bed, but he could not speak. If one had cared to look into his eyes they might have seen them full of tears.

Quantrell, by the dim light of a single candle, recognized James, smiled and held out his hand, and said to him very gently, though a little reproachfully: "Why did you come back? The enemy are thick about you here; they are passing every hour."

"To see if you were alive or dead, Captain. If the first, to save you; if the last, to put you in a grave."

"I thank you very much, Frank, but why try to take me away? I am cold below the hips. I can neither ride, walk nor crawl; I am dead and yet I am alive."

Frank James went to the door and called in Parmer, Ross and Hulse. Quantrell recognized them all in his old, calm, quiet fashion, and bade them wipe away their tears, for they were crying visibly.

Then Frank James, joined in his entreaties by the entreaties of his comrades, pleaded with Quantrell for permission to carry him away to the mountains of Nelson County by slow and easy stages, each swearing to guard him hour by hour until he recovered or died over his body, defending it to the last. He knew that every pledge made by them would be kept to the death. He felt that every word spoken was a golden word and meant absolute devotion. His faith in their affection was as steadfast and abiding as of old. He listened until they had done talking, with the old staid courtesy of victorious Guerrilla days, and then he silenced them with an answer which, from its resoluteness, they knew to be unalterable.

"I cannot live. I have run a long time; I have come out unhurt from many desperate places; I have fought to kill and I have killed; I regret nothing. The end is close at hand. I am resting easy here and will die so. You do not know how your devotion has touched my heart, nor can you understand how grateful I am for the love you have shown me. Try and get back to your homes, and avoid if you can the perils that beset you."

Until 10 o'clock the next day these men remained with Quantrell. He talked with them very freely of the past, but never of the earlier life in Kansas. Many messages were sent to absent friends, and much good advice was given touching the surrender of the remnant of the band. Again and again he returned to the earlier struggles in Missouri and dwelt long over the recollections and the reminiscences of the first two years of Guerrilla warfare.

Finally the parting came, and those who looked last upon Quantrell's face that morning as they stooped to tell him goodbye, looked their last upon it forever.

Terrill had promised Quantrell positively that he should not be removed from Wakefield's house, but in three days he had either forgotten his promise or had deliberately broken his pledge. He informed General Palmer, commanding the department of Kentucky, of the facts of the fight, and of the desperate character of the wounded officer left paralyzed behind him, suggesting at the same time the advisability of having him removed to a place of safety.

General Palmer sent an ambulance under a heavy escort to Wakefield's house and Quantrell, suffering greatly and scarcely more alive than dead, was hauled to the military hospital in Louisville and deposited there.

Until the question of recovery had been absolutely decided against him, but few friends were permitted into his presence. If any one conversed with him at all, the conversation of necessity was required to be carried on in the presence of an official. Mrs. Ross visited him thus—Christian woman, devoted to the South, and of active and practical patriotism—and took some dying messages to loved and true ones in Missouri.

Mrs. Ross left him at one o'clock in the afternoon and at four the next afternoon the great Guerrilla died.

His passing away, after a life so singularly fitful and tempestuous, was as the passing of a summer cloud. He had been asleep, and as he awoke he called for water. A Sister of Charity at the bedside put a glass of water to his lips, but he did not drink. She heard him murmur once audibly—"Boys, get ready." Then a long pause, then one word more—"Steady!" and then when she drew back from bending over the murmuring man, she fell upon her knees and prayed. Quantrell was dead.

Before his death he had become a Catholic and had been visited daily by two old priests. To one of these he made confession, and such a confession! He told everything. He was too serious and earnest a man to do less. He kept nothing back, not even the least justifiable of his many homicides.

As the priest listened and listened, and as year after year of the wild war work was made to give up its secrets, what manner of a man must the priest have imagined lay dying there.

Let history be just. On that hospital bed, watched by the calm, colorless face of a Sister of Charity, a dead man lay who, when living, had filled with his deeds four years of terrible war history. A singularly placid look had come with the great change. Alike was praise or censure, reward or punishment. Fate had done its worst and the future stood revealed to the spirit made omniscient by its journey through the Valley of the Shadow of Death. He had done with summer's heat and winter's cold, with spectral ambuscades and midnight vigils. There would never be any war in the land of the hereafter. The swoop of cavalry, the roar of combat, the agony of defeat, white faces trampled by the iron hoofs of horses, the march—the bivouac, the battle; what remains of these when the transfiguration was done and when the river called Jordan rolled between the shores of the finite and the infinite? Nothing! And yet by those, standing or falling, must the great Guerrilla be judged.

Quantrell differed in some degree from every Guerrilla who was either a comrade or his contemporary. Not superior to Todd in courage and enterprise, nor to Haller, Poole, Jarrette, Younger, Taylor, Anderson, Frank James, Gregg, Lea, Maddox, Dan Vaughn, or Yager, he yet had one peculiar quality which none of these save Gregg, Frank James, Thrailkill, Lea and Younger possessed to the same pre-eminent degree—extraordinary resource and cunning.

All the Guerrillas fought. Indeed, at certain times and under certain conditions fighting might justly have been considered the least of their accomplishments. A successful leader requires coolness, intrepidity, robust health, fine horsemanship, expert pistol practice, quick perception in peril, great rapidity of movement, immense activity, and inexorable fixedness of purpose.

Those mentioned excelled in these qualities, but at times they were too eager to fight, took too many desperate chances, or rushed too recklessly into combats where they could not win. Quantrell counted the cost of everything; watched every way lest an advantage should be taken of him; sought to shield and save his men; strove by much strategy to have the odds with rather than against him; traveled a multitude of long roads rather than one short one once too often; took upon himself many disguises to prevent an embarrassing familiarity; retreat often rather than fight and be worsted; kept scouts everywhere; had the faculty of divination to an almost occult degree; believed in young men; paid attention to small things; listened to every man's advice and then took his own; stood by his soldiers; obeyed strictly the law of retaliation; preferred the old dispensation to the new—that is to say, the code of Moses to the code of Jesus Christ; inculcated by precept and example the self abnegation and devotion to comrade; fought desperately; carried a black flag; killed everything; made the idea of surrender ridiculous; snapped his fingers at death; was something of a fatalist; rarely drank; trusted few women, but these with his life; played high at cards; believed in religion; respected its ordinances; went at intervals to church; understood human nature thoroughly; never quarreled; was generally taciturn and one of the coolest and deadliest men in a personal combat known to the border. He rode like he was carved from the horse beneath him. In an organization where skill with a pistol was a passport to leadership he shot with a revolver as Leatherstocking shot with a rifle. He drilled his men to fight equally with either hand. Fairly matched, God help the column that came in contact with him.

As to the kind of warfare Quantrell waged, that is another matter. Like the war of La Vendee, the Guerrilla war was one rather of hatred than of opinion. The regular Confederates were fighting for a cause and a nationality—the Guerrilla for vengeance. Mementoes of murdered kinsmen mingled with their weapons; vows consecrated the act of enlistment and the cry for blood was heard from homestead to homestead. Quantrell became a Guerrilla because he had been most savagely dealt with, and he became a chief because he had prudence, firmness, courage, audacity and common sense. In personal intrepidity he was inferior to no man. His features were pleasing without being handsome, his eyes were blue and penetrating. He had a Roman nose. In height he was five feet, eleven inches, and his form was well knit, graceful and sinewy. His constitution was vigorous, and his physical endurance equal to an Indian. His glance was rapid and unerring. His judgment was clearest and surest when the responsibility was heaviest, and when the difficulties gathered thickest about him. Based upon skill, energy, perspicacity and unusual presence of mind, his fame as a Guerrilla will endure for generations.

Quantrell died a Catholic and was buried in a Catholic cemetery at Louisville, Kentucky.

THE YOUNGERS AND JAMESES AFTER THE WAR

THE end of the war also brought an end to armed resistance by the Guerrillas. As an organization, they never fought again. The most of them kept their weapons; and a few of them had great need to keep them. Some were killed because of the terrible renown won in the four years' war; some were forced to hide themselves in the unknown of the outlying territories, and some were persecuted and driven into desperate defiance and resistance because they were human and intrepid. To this latter class the Jameses and Youngers belonged.

No men ever strove harder to put the past behind them. No men ever submitted more sincerely to the results of a war that had as many excesses on one side as on the other. No men ever went to work with a heartier good will to keep good faith with society and make themselves amenable to the law. No men ever sacrificed more for peace, and for the bare privilege of doing just as hundreds like them had done—the privilege of going back again into the obscurity of civil life and becoming again a part of the enterprising economy of the commonwealth. They were not permitted so to do, try how they would, and as hard, and as patiently.

After the death of Quantrell and the surrender of the remnant of his Guerrillas, Frank James was not permitted, at first, to return to Missouri at all, much less to his home in Clay County.

He lingered in Clay County as long as possible, very circumspect in his actions and very conservative in his behavior. Tempted one day by his beardless face and innocent walk and to bear upon him roughly, four Federal soldiers set upon Frank James in Brandenburg and made haste to force an issue. For a moment the old fire of his earlier and stormier days flared up all of a sudden from the ashes of the past and consumed as with a single hot blast of passion prudence, accountability, caution and discretion. He fought as he had fought at Centralia. Two of the Federals were killed instantly, the third was desperately wounded, while the fourth shot Frank badly in the joint of the left hip, inflicting a grievous hurt and one which caused him afterwards a great deal of pain and trouble.

Staunch friends hid him while the hue and cry were heaviest, and careful surgical attention brought him back to life when he lay so close to death's door that by the lifting of a hand he also might have lifted its latch.

This fight, however, was not one of his own seeking, nor one which he could have avoided without the exhibition of a quality he never had known anything about and never could know anything about—physical cowardice.

Jesse James, emaciated, tottering as he walked, fighting what seemed to everyone a hopeless battle—of "the skeleton boy against skeleton death"—joined his mother in Nebraska and returned with her to their home near Kearney, in Clay County. His wound would not heal, and more ominous still, every now and then there was a hemorrhage.

In the spring of 1866 he was just barely able to mount a horse and ride a bit. And he did ride, but he rode armed, watchful, vigilant, haunted. He might be killed, waylaid, ambuscaded, assassinated; but he would be killed with his eyes open and his pistols about him.

The hunt for this maimed and emaciated Guerrilla culminated on the night of February 18th, 1867. On this night an effort was made to kill him. Five militiamen, well armed and mounted, came to his mother's house and demanded admittance. The weather was bitterly cold, and Jesse James, parched with fever, was tossing wearily in bed. His pistols were under his head. His step-father. Dr. Samuels, heard the militiamen as they walked upon the front porch, and demanded to know what they wanted. They told him to open the door. He came up to Jesse's room and asked him what he should do. "Help me to the window," was the low, calm reply, "that I may look out." He did so.

There was snow on the ground and the moon was shining. He saw that all the horses hitched to the fence had on cavalry saddles, and then he knew that the men were soldiers. He had but one of two things to do—drive them away or die.

Incensed at the step-father's silence, they were hammering at the door with the butts of their muskets and calling out to Jesse to come down stairs, swearing that they knew he was in the house, and that they would have him out, dead or alive.

He went down stairs softly, having first dressed himself, crept close up to the front door and listened until from the talk of the men he thought he was able to get a fairly accurate pistol range. Then he put a heavy dragoon pistol to within three inches of the upper panel of the door and fired. A man cried out and fell. Before the surprise was off he threw the door wide open, and with a pistol in each hand began a rapid fusillade. A second man was killed as he ran, two men were wounded severely, and surrendered, while the fifth marauder, terrified, yet unhurt, rushed swiftly to his horse and escaped in the darkness.

What else could Jesse James have done? In those evil days bad men in bands were doing bad things continually in the name of the law, order and vigilance committees.

He had been a desperate Guerrilla; he had fought under a black flag, he had made a name for terrible prowess along the border; he had survived dreadful wounds; it was known that he would fight at any hour or in any way; he could not be frightened out from his native county; he could be neither intimidated nor robbed, and hence the wanton war waged upon Jesse and Frank James, and this is the reason they became outlaws, and hence the reason also that—outlaws as they were and proscribed in county, or state or territory—they had more friends than the officers who hunted them, and more defenders than the armed men who sought to secure their bodies, dead or alive.

The future of the Youngers after the war was similar to the Jameses. Cole was in California when the surrender came, and he immediately accepted the situation. He returned to Missouri, determined to forget the past, and fixed in his purpose to reunite the scattered members of his once prosperous and happy family, and prepare and make comfortable a home for his stricken and suffering mother.

Despite everything that has been said and written of this man, he was, during all the border warfare, a generous and merciful man. Others killed and that in any form or guise or fashion; he alone in open and honorable battle. His heart was always kind, and his sympathies always easily aroused. He not only took prisoners himself, but he treated them afterwards as prisoners, and released them to rejoin commands that spared nothing alive of Guerrilla associations that fell into their hands.

He was the oldest son, and all the family looked up to him. His mother had been driven out of Cass County into Jackson, out of Jackson into Lafayette, and out of Lafayette into Jackson again. Not content with butchering the father in cold blood, the ravenous cut-throats and thieves followed the mother with a malignity unparalleled. Every house she owned or inhabited was burnt, every outbuilding, every rail, every straw stack, every corn pen, every pound of food and every store of forage. Her stock was stolen. Her household goods were even appropriated. She had no place to lay her head that could be called her own, and but for the kindness and Christianity of her devoted neighbors, she must have suffered greatly.

At this time Coleman and James returned to Missouri and went hopefully and bravely to work. Their father's land remained to them. That at least had neither been set fire to nor hauled away in wagons, nor driven into Kansas.

Western Missouri was then full of disbanded Federal soldiers, organized squads of predatory Redlegs and Jayhawkers, horse thieves disguised as vigilance committees, and highway robbers known as law and order men.

In addition, Drake's constitution disfranchised every property owner along the border. An honest man could not officially stand between the helpless of his community and the imported lazzaroni who preyed upon them; a decent man's voice could not be heard above the clamor of the beggars quarreling over stolen plunder; and a just man's expostulations penetrated never into the councils of the chief scoundrels who planned the murders and the robberies.

Coleman Younger's work was like the work of a pioneer in the wilderness, but he did it as became the hardy descendants of a stalwart race of pioneers. He cut logs and built a comfortable log house for his mother. He made rails and fenced in his land. In lieu of horses or mules, he plowed with oxen. He stayed steadfastly at home. He heard rumors of threats being made against his life, but he paid no attention to them. He took part in no political meetings. He tried to hide himself and be forgotten.

The bloodhounds were on his track, however, and swore either to kill him or drive him from the country. A vigilance committee composed of skulking murderers and red-handed robbers went one night to surprise the two brothers and end the hunt with a massacre. Forewarned, James and Coleman fled. The family were wantonly insulted, and a younger brother, John, a mere boy, was brutally beaten and then hung until life was almost extinct. This was done to force him to tell the whereabouts of James and Coleman.

Mrs. Younger never entirely recovered from the shock of that night's work, lingering along hopelessly yet patiently for several months and finally dying in the full assurance of the Christian's blessed hereafter.

The death of this persecuted woman, however, did not end the persecution. Cole Younger was repeatedly waylaid and fired at. His stock was killed through mere deviltry, or driven off to swell the gains of insatiable wolves. His life was in hourly jeopardy, as was the life of his brother James. They plowed in the fields as men who saw suspended above them a naked sword blade. They permitted no light to be lit in the house at night. They traveled the public highway warily. They were hunted men and proscribed men in the midst of their own people. They were chased away from their premises by armed men. Once Cole was badly wounded by the bullet of an assassin. Once, half dressed, he had to flee for his life. If he made a crop, he was not permitted to gather it and when something of a success might have come to him after the expenditure of so much toil, energy, long-suffering and forbearance, he was not let alone in peace long enough to utilize his returns and make out of his resources their legitimate gains.

Of course there could be but one ending to all this long and unbroken series of malignant persecutions, lying-in-wait, midnight surprises, perpetual robbings, and most villainous assaults and attempted murders—Coleman and James Younger left home and left Jackson County. They buckled on their pistols and rode away to Texas, resolved from that time on to protect themselves, to fight when they were attacked, and to make it so hot for the assassins and the detectives who were eternally on their track that by and by the contract taken to murder them would be a contract not particularly conducive to steady investments. They were hounded to it.

They endured every species of insult and attack, and would have still continued to endure it in silence and almost non-resistance if such forbearance had mitigated in any manner the virulence of their enemies, or brought any nearer to an appeasement the merciless fate which seemed to be eternally at their heels. The peaceful pursuits of life were denied them. The law which should have protected them was overridden. Indeed, there was no law. The courts were instruments of plunder. The civil officers were cutthroats. Instead of a legal process, there was a vigilance committee. Men were hung because of a very natural desire to keep hold of their own property. To the cruel vigor of actual war, there had succeeded the irresponsible despotism of greedy highwaymen buttressed upon assassination. The border counties were overrun with bands of predatory plunderers. Some Confederate soldiers dared not return home and many Guerrillas fled the country. It was dark everywhere, and the bravest held their breath, not knowing how much longer they would be permitted to remain peacefully at home, or suffered to enjoy the fruits of the labors they had endured.

Fortunately for all, however, the well nigh extinct embers of a merciless border war were not blown upon long enough and persistently enough to kindle another conflagration.

But neither the Jameses nor the Youngers had been permitted to rest long at any one time since the surrender of the Confederate armies. Some dastardly deeds had been done against them, too, in the name of the law. Take for example, Pinkerton's midnight raid upon the house of Mrs. Zerelda Samuels, mother of the James boys. The family was wrapped in profound sleep. Only women and children were about the premises, and an old man long past his prime. The cowards—how many is not accurately known, probably a dozen—crept close to this house through the midnight, surrounded it, found its inmates asleep, and threw into the kitchen where an old negress was in bed with her children, a lighted hand grenade, wrapped about with flannel saturated with turpentine. The lurid light from this inflammable fluid awakened the negro woman and she in turn awakened the sleeping whites. They rushed to subdue the flames and save their property. Children were gathered together in the kitchen, little things, helpless and terrified. All of a sudden there was a terrible explosion. Mrs. Samuels' right arm was blown off above the elbow, a bright little boy, eight years old, had his bowels torn out. Dr. Samuels was seriously cut and hurt, the old negro woman was maimed, and several of the other children more or less injured. The hand grenade had done its work, and there had been a tragedy performed by men calling themselves civilized, in the midst of a peaceful community and upon a helpless family of women and children and what would have disgraced Nero or made some of the monstrous murders of Diocletian was as white is to black. Yet Pinkerton's paid assassins did this because his paid assassins knew better how to kill women and children than armed men in open combat.

Dear Reader, what would you have done under the same circumstances? Put yourself in the Jameses' and Youngers' places, and think it over.

When Jesse James was killed at St. Joseph, Missouri, Governor Crittenden, then governor of the state of Missouri, wired me to know if I would go up and identify him.

I wired him I would, providing I could go armed.

He answered, "Perfectly satisfactory to me. Meet me at Union Station, Kansas City, Missouri, tomorrow morning."

I secured several of my old Guerrilla friends to accompany the Governor and myself to St. Joseph, Missouri, unbeknown to the Governor, however, for I did not know how I stood with the people at St. Joseph. I was just playing safety first. I met the Governor at the depot. He asked me what attitude I thought Frank James would take towards him for offering a reward and having Jesse killed. I told him "If Frank wanted to kill him for revenge, he surely would."

He looked pale, but not half so pale as he did the day Frank surrendered. A heavy reward hanging over Frank James' head, he made his way past the guards and sergeant-at-arms, stationed at the Governor's mansion at Jefferson City, the capital of Missouri, and surrendered to Governor Crittenden in his office. On entering his office, Frank said:

"Is this Governor Crittenden?"

"Yes," was the reply.

"This is Frank James. I came to surrender," at the same time pulling two heavy dragoon pistols and handing them to the Governor. "Here are arms, Governor, but not all I have, nor will I give them up until I know you will give me protection."

Frank told me afterwards that "Governor Crittenden's face will never be whiter when he is dead than it was the day I surrendered."

I identified Jesse James at St. Joseph, Missouri, to the Governor's entire satisfaction. Since then it has been said that Jesse was still alive and that it was a wax figure that was buried, but this is all a lie.

There is one good act the James boys did while they were outlaws.

A southern widow woman some time soon after the war had mortgaged her farm to an old Redleg who had moved from Lawrence, Kansas, to Kansas City.

When the loan expired he drove out to see her and informed her that if she did not have the money by ten o'clock the next morning he would foreclose.

Soon after he had left, up rode Jesse and Frank James, and found the lady crying and taking on. They inquired what was wrong, and she related the whole story.

Frank said, "You send your son in the morning and tell the old Federal to bring all releases and all papers fully signed and you will pay him in full. Jesse and I will let you have the money."

Next morning the boy went with the message, and in the evening out came the old Federal in his bus with his negro driver, drove up to the house, went in, and the lady paid him in full with cash, getting all releases and papers fixed up. The old man bowed and scraped and, tipping his hat, said, "Goodbye, lady," and he and his "nigger" driver started back to Kansas City. When but a few hundred yards or so from the house and close to a ravine, Jesse and Frank held him up and relieved him of the money they had loaned the lady, together with all the rest he had for interest.

During the World War, in conversation with friends, I told them to take away from Germany her airplanes, gases and machine guns, and if it were possible to call Quantrell's old band together, of which at no time were there over three hundred and fifty men, all told, under Todd, Poole, Yager, Anderson, Younger, Jarrett, Haller, Quantrell and myself, I could take these three hundred and fifty men and go to Berlin in a gallop, for history does not now and never will know the power there was in the Quantrell band. It has been given up long ago that they were the most fighting devils the world has ever known or ever will know.

THE END.

Lector House believes that a society develops through a two-fold approach of continuous learning and adaptation, which is derived from the study of classic literary works spread across the historic timeline of literature records. Therefore, we aim at reviving, repairing and redeveloping all those inaccessible or damaged but historically as well as culturally important literature across subjects so that the future generations may have an opportunity to study and learn from past works to embark upon a journey of creating a better future.

This book is a result of an effort made by Lector House towards making a contribution to the preservation and repair of original ancient works which might hold historical significance to the approach of continuous learning across subjects.

HAPPY READING & LEARNING!

LECTOR HOUSE LLP
E-MAIL: info@lectorhouse.com

Printed by Libri Plureos GmbH in Hamburg,
Germany